55
HIKES around™

SNOQUALMIE PASS
MOUNTAINS-TO-SOUND
GREENWAY

55 HIKES around ™

SNOQUALMIE PASS
MOUNTAINS–TO–SOUND GREENWAY

SECOND EDITION

Harvey Manning
Photos by Ira Spring

THE
MOUNTAINEERS
BOOKS

Published by
The Mountaineers Books
1001 SW Klickitat Way, Suite 201
Seattle, WA 98134

© 1993, 2001 by Harvey Manning and Ira Spring

First edition published in 1993 as *Hiking the Mountains to Sound Greenway*
Second edition: first printing 2001, second printing 2001, third printing 2002,
fourth printing 2003

Published simultaneously in Great Britain by Cordee, 3a DeMontfort Street,
Leicester, England, LE1 7HD

Manufactured in the United States of America

Project Editor: Kathleen Cubley
Editor: Kris Fulsaas
Cover and Book Design: The Mountaineers Books
Layout Artist: Gray Mouse Graphics
Cartographer: Gray Mouse Graphics
All photographs by Ira Spring unless otherwise noted

Cover photograph: *Snow Lake Trail, Alpine Lakes Wilderness* © Bob and Ira
Spring
Frontispiece: *Pacific Crest Trail crossing the Kendall Katwalk*

Library of Congress Cataloging-in-Publication Data

Manning, Harvey.
    55 hikes around Snoqualmie Pass : mountains to Sound Greenway / by
  Harvey Manning; photographs by Ira Spring.-- 1st ed.
      p. cm.
      Includes bibliographical references.
      ISBN 0-89886-777-0 (pbk.)
      1. Hiking--Washington (State)--Snoqualmie Pass Region--Guidebooks.
  2. Snoqualmie Pass Region (Wash.)--Guidebooks.   I. Title: Fifty-five hikes
  around Snoqualmie Pass. II. Title.
  GV199.42.W22 S566 2001
  917.95'7--dc21

                                                        2001000036

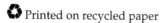

CONTENTS

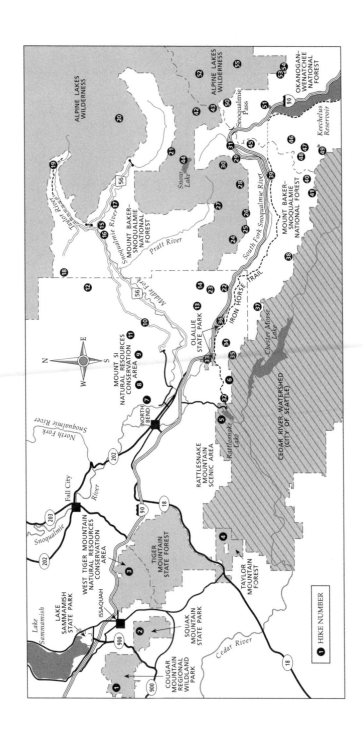

Forest trail on Cougar Mountain (Hike 1)

QUICK TRAIL FINDER

EASY TRAILS LESS THAN 2 MILES (EACH WAY) AND NOT MORE THAN 500 FEET ELEVATION GAIN

Asahel Curtis Nature Trail	Elevation gain 180 feet	Hike 39
Cougar Mountain	Elevation gain 200 feet	Hike 1
Denny Creek Slippery Slab	Elevation gain 500 feet	Hike 29
Franklin Falls	Elevation gain 200 feet	Hike 31
Gold Creek Pond	Elevation gain none	Hike 51
Lodge Lake	Elevation gain 500 feet in, 375 feet out	Hike 45
Olallie State Park	Elevation gain 210 feet	Hike 36
Rainy Creek Pool	Unmaintained trail	Hike 16
Tradition Lake	Elevation gain none	Hike 3
Twin Lake	Elevation gain 200 feet	Hike 47
Twin Falls	Elevation gain 500 feet	Hike 33
Wildside Trail–Red Town Trail	Elevation gain 200 feet	Hike 1

MODERATE TRAILS LESS THAN 5 MILES (EACH WAY) AND NOT MORE THAN 1000 FEET ELEVATION GAIN

CCC Road-Trail West	Elevation gain 400 feet	Hike 10
CCC Road-Trail	Elevation gain 410 feet	Hike 10
Cedar Butte	Elevation gain 900 feet	Hike 6
Middle Fork Snoqualmie River	Elevation gain 300 feet	Hike 17
Mirror Lake	Elevation gain 800 feet	Hike 49
Mt. Gardner	Elevation gain 1000 feet	Hike 38
Mount Si Big View Cliffs	Elevation gain 850 feet	Hike 8
Otter Falls, Lipsy Lake, and Big Creek Falls	Elevation gain 650 feet	Hike 19

LONGER HIKES

Annette Lake	Elevation gain 1400 feet	Hike 40
CCC Road-Trail to end	Elevation gain 570 feet	Hike 10
Dirty Harry's Balcony	Elevation gain 1300 feet	Hike 22

Hester Lake	Elevation gain 2500 feet	Hike 20
Iron Horse Trail end to end	Elevation gain 1500 feet	Hike 32
Kendall Peak Lakes	Elevation gain 2100 feet	Hike 50
Little Si	Elevation gain 1200 feet	Hike 7
Margaret Lake	Elevation gain 1300 feet in, 300 feet out	Hike 54
Middle Fork to Pratt River	Unmaintained; easy to lose	Hike 16
Mount Catherine	Elevation gain 1300 feet	Hike 46
Mt. Gardner	Elevation gain 1500 feet	Hike 38
Mt. Margaret	Elevation gain 1500 feet in, 600 feet out	Hike 53
Mount Si	Elevation gain 3200 feet	Hike 8
Myrtle Lake	Elevation gain 2400 feet	Hike 20
Quartz Creek–Lake Blethen	Elevation gain 2000 feet	Hike 18
Rattlesnake Ledge	Elevation gain 1160 feet	Hike 5
Rock Creek	Elevation gain 2800 feet	Hike 21
Silver Peak Loop	Elevation gain 1500 feet	Hike 48
Snag Flat	Elevation gain 1350 feet	Hike 8
Snow Lake	Elevation gain 1300 feet in, 400 feet out	Hike 44
Talapus and Olallie Lakes	Elevation gain 1220 feet	Hike 26
Taylor Mountain	Elevation gain 1450 feet	Hike 4
Tiger Mountain Trail	Elevation gain 2100 feet	Hike 3
West Tiger 3	Elevation gain 2000 feet	Hike 3

STRENUOUS HIKES WITH A LOT OF ELEVATION GAIN

Bandera Mountain	Elevation gain 2850 feet	Hike 25
Central Peak–Eastside Loop	Elevation gain 1300 feet	Hike 2
Commonwealth Basin	Elevation gain 2700 feet in, 250 feet out	Hike 42
Dirty Harry's Peak	Elevation gain 3400 feet	Hike 23
Gold Creek	Elevation gain 1600 feet	Hike 52
Granite Lakes	Elevation gain 2300 feet	Hike 14
Granite Mountain	Elevation gain 3800 feet	Hike 28
Green Mountain	Elevation gain 1950 feet	Hike 11

Kendall Katwalk	Elevation gain 2700 feet in, 300 feet out	Hike 43
Lake Lillian	Elevation gain 1750 feet in, 750 feet out	Hike 53
Mailbox Peak	Elevation gain 4000 feet	Hike 13
Mason Lake	Elevation gain 2000 feet	Hike 24
McClellan Butte	Elevation gain 3700 feet	Hike 37
Melakwa Lake	Elevation gain 2600 feet in, 350 feet out	Hike 30
Mt. Defiance	Elevation gain 3500 feet	Hike 24
Mt. Teneriffe	Difficult; elevation gain 4000 feet	Hike 9
Mt. Washington	Elevation gain 3400 feet	Hike 35
Owl Hike Spot	Elevation gain 1600 feet	Hike 34
Pratt Lake Saddle	Elevation gain 2300 feet in, 700 feet out	Hike 27
Rachel Lake	Elevation gain 1600 feet	Hike 55
Red Pass	Elevation gain 2700 feet in, 250 feet out	Hike 42
Scout Lake–Silver Peak Loop	Elevation gain 3300 feet	Hike 41
South Bessemer Mountain	Elevation gain 4200 feet	Hike 12
Stegosaurus Butte	Elevation gain 1070 feet	Hike 15

From Granite Mountain trail (Hike 28)

FOREWORD

Most hikers don't leave home without Harvey and Ira's trail bible in their pack, but some may not know the visionary role played by Harvey Manning as an early advocate for a greenway from the Cascades to Puget Sound. He preached that a "wilderness on the Metro" could be created along Interstate 90, and today his sermon is taking shape in the Mountains-to-Sound Greenway.

Collaborative and cooperative efforts toward this vision grew strongly in the 1990s. After substantial investments by purchase and exchange, "we the people" now own key parts of the Greenway, to be managed for us as forests by federal, state, and local governments. Hard work by many citizens and gutsy decisions by public officials now ensure that this accessible corridor will always be more than a few patches of trees in a sea of streets and buildings. Along the forks of the Snoqualmie River, on the Issaquah Alps, on Rattlesnake Ridge and Mount Si, green blankets of growing forests will continue to welcome the children and grandchildren of today's hikers. The main trails and vistas of the Greenway can be shared by people of all incomes and physical abilities.

As you walk these trails, stop every so often to feel the quiet pulse of the planet. Minutes away from the push and jostle of metropolis, the forest invites you to a different kind of real world. Accept the peace that comes with the sound of forest streams. The common bonds between people and nature are rooted in primal connections. Trees make the oxygen we inhale and consume the carbon dioxide we exhale.

This book is a guide to hundreds of neat surprises. Don't be astonished at the beauty you can find so close to home. Centuries-old firs and cedars stand watch along the Twin Falls gorge minutes from North Bend. Along Greenway hillsides, the scars of logging roads are being healed and thousands of acres of second growth are growing to maturity. In 1998, I-90 became the only interstate freeway in the United States to be designated a National Scenic Byway™.

Don't be afraid of a mixture of preserves and working forests. Some trees on public land will be harvested selectively on a perpetual-yield basis to furnish lumber for homes, money for schools, and open grazing areas for deer and elk.

If we keep our wits about us, the Mountains-to-Sound Greenway can help serve human needs in a sustainable society. But this can happen only if we learn to balance the economic and natural uses of the forest, if we remember that trails and scenic viewpoints need continuing loving care, and if we recognize that such care means ongoing work by volunteers and money from fees and taxes. Finally, if we *never* let these forests be converted to buildings, then this book can guide happy hikers through a green world for a long time to come.

Jim Ellis
April 15, 2000

(Jim Ellis has served as president of the Mountains-to-Sound Greenway Trust since its founding in 1990. The Trust is a private not-for-profit Washington corporation.)

HARVEY'S PREFACE

George Borrow, author of the classic *Wild Wales*, published in 1862, was asked by friends why he did not expedite his explorations by taking the railroad. He answered, "I am fond of the beauties of nature. It is impossible to see much of the beauties of nature unless you walk."

As a younger climber I knew an older climber who as a younger climber had known an older climber who as a younger climber had shouldered his Yukon pack at North Bend to set out for peaks at Snoqualmie Pass. That was about the time of the Guggenheim Trophy Race from New York to the 1908 Alaska-Yukon-Pacific (AYP) Exposition in Seattle. Wheels, on automobiles as well as on wagons, were then becoming a more or less frequent alternative to feet, "if'n the Lord was willin' and the creek don't rise."

Mine was the first generation that might be said to have traveled more by wheels than feet—the baby carriage, the kiddy car, the Keene Coaster, the family sedan (my folks' generation being the first to routinely enjoy such ownership). My folks also lived during the salad days of the First Great Big Bicycle Craze ("Daisy, Daisy . . . You'll look sweet upon the seat of a bicycle built for two"). As a country kid I hardly ever left the yard except on a bike, and what with going to school and Scout meetings, fetching groceries, and years of doing a 12-mile paper route, I pedaled some 10,000 miles.

But on a spring morning of the sort when Swedes, after the long winter night, run out in the sun, take off their clothes, jump in the lake, and make movies, there came a foreshadowing. While mounting my bike for the 10mph ride to school on the county road, my eyes were drawn to the 2mph trail over the field, through the flowers and birdsongs, into the woods. After that I never biked to school except when late getting up.

Soren Kierkegaard, the Danish philosopher, said in the 1840s, "Most men pursue pleasure with such breathless haste that they hurry past it." Most of the millions of Americans who hurtle at 70mph back and forth along I-90 ("The Main Street of the Northwest") are on business, not pleasure, nor would the bullying by other hurtlers permit them to loiter at 50mph, the limit temporarily imposed during the First Great Big Oil Shortage of a quarter century ago, much less the 28mph that was the cruising speed of my personal vehicle from 1941 to 1948, a 1930 Model A Ford.

Our subject in this book is not business and thus has nothing to do with 70mph. Nor do we take more than a sidelong scowl at the Futurist Manifesto announced at the start of the twentieth century, which exulted: "Hurrah for speedy machines! Race cars, airplanes! No more contact with vile earth! FASTER THINGS FOR FASTER LIVING!" In his end-of-the-century novel *Slowness*, Milan Kundera asked, "Why has the pleasure of slowness disappeared? Ah, where have they gone—the amblers of yesteryear? Have they vanished with the footpaths, with Nature? There is a Czech proverb that describes their easy indolence: 'They are gazing at God's windows.'"

The Futurist movement lost its top generals in 1945—though, to be sure, the army hurtles on. Kundera was too pessimistic, because the mean speed of this book is 2mph, and plenty of God's windows remain wide open.

Ira and I know well the windows along what is now the Mountains-to-Sound Greenway. Though the Olympics were our home hills, our introduction on Boy Scout hikes to mountain wildlands, Mount Rainier was always for both of us *The* Mountain, and we could not but become familiar with the Main Street. This book therefore, in addition to lessons in geography, has an historical dimension, because the two of us are, willy-nilly, not a whole lot younger than the Main Street.

Denny Creek Slippery Slab (Hike 29)

In 1977 I noted on the map a primitive road, paralleling the paved highway, up from the North Bend Plain to the crest of Grouse Ridge, the terminal moraine of the Puget Lobe of the Cordilleran Ice Sheet. A friend at King County Parks informed me that this was not a log-haul road privately owned by a timber company (though it was treated as such by the company) but a public road, the very first road from the lowlands to Snoqualmie Pass.

Seattle pioneers made a start at the road's construction in 1859, aborted by the Civil War. In 1865 boosters subscribed $2,500 to clear a Snoqualmie Pass Trail–Wagon Road, and this was extended nearly to the pass, though actual crossings were so rare that one made in 1872 rated newspaper attention. The government proving apathetic, in 1883 A. A. Denny and H. L. Yesler rallied fellow townboomers to a demonstration of that good ol' "Seattle Spirit," and their Seattle–Walla Walla Train and Wagon Road Company opened the Seattle–Walla Walla Toll Road, the first dependable cross-Cascades wheelway. There was little call for it when built, less after completion of the Northern Pacific Railroad through Stampede Pass, and in 1892 the 6.2 miles of 14-foot right-of-way up Grouse Ridge were signed over to King County. Trees fell, creeks gullied, weeds grew. But time was marching (wheeling) on and in 1905 the first cars crossed Snoqualmie Pass, helped here and there by ferry, teams of horses, and shoulders to the wheel. The 1909 automobile race from New York to Seattle gave the race route a boost. Soon everybody was Sunday-driving in Model Ts and Merry Oldsmobiles, a nation of Barney Oldfields and Mr. Toads (of Toad Hall).

In 1913 a primary transcontinental highway was officially plotted on the map over Snoqualmie Pass. Formally opened in 1915, this Sunset Highway bypassed Grouse Ridge, choosing instead the riverside line that remained in use as US Highway 10 until the completion of General Eisenhower's Interstate 90 in the 1970s. From 1931 it was kept open in winter, sort of.

On a day in 1977, ascending the 1865 wagon road, I stopped near the crest of Grouse Ridge. Below sprawled the North Bend Plain, bed of a Pleistocene lake. At its south edge, to my left, ran the South Fork Snoqualmie River, close to the base of Rattlesnake Mountain; behind me, above the moraine, the stream valley carried the Main Street. At the north edge, to my right, ran the Middle Fork, close by the base of Mount Si; above the moraine, its valley was the "Center Ring." Just past Si, at North Bend, the North Fork completed the river, which then fell off the plain in Snoqualmie Falls and made its bend north to join the Skykomish River.

My eye (of the now) fell on the multiple concrete lanes of I-90, rose to forests (and tree mines) on the valley walls, and traced Main Street west into the smog of Puget Sound City.

My ear (on the past) heard wagon wheels of immigrants. Mooing and baaing of beef and mutton walking from the Okanogan Valley to butcher shops in Seattle. *Putt-putt-bang* of AYP road-racers. Mutterings of Original Inhabitants on the way to the Seattle stockade, where they would stand behind trees for shelter from the U.S. Navy ship-of-war firing cannon balls from Elliott Bay, and holler at the real estate speculators in the stockade, "Why don't you go back where you came from?" The glacier dropping boulders from Canada.

The Spring family crossed Snoqualmie Pass in 1927, completing a three-week journey over the continent-spanning highways, still largely incomplete and irregularly maintained; Ira was too young, and his family had altogether too many adventures, for him to retain any memory of the pass. The Manning family crossed the summer of 1932 in our flight east from the Seattle Depression to the Lowell Depression, and recrossed the summer of 1933 in our flight west, preferring to starve at home. I also was too young, and the width of North America too full of sandstorms, prairie fires, detours, and rattlesnakes for the pass to stand out; I guess we should have stopped there, as we did at the sign that announced "Continental Divide," to give thanks for our safe escape.

From my early life in Seattle I do fondly recall Maloney's Grove, east of North Bend, where we often camped; in the 1970s I was surprised and delighted to discover a road going off I-90 and dead-ending at the South Fork, signed "Maloney Grove Road." The swings and teeter-totters were long gone but the river was rolling on and on as before. Snoqualmie Falls, of course, was obligatory for relatives visiting from Massachusetts; my shining memory there was in the depths of the Depression when Uncle Ratch, well employed all through those starveling years, bought me a banana split, my first.

Playgrounds and ice cream are history on the personal level; I also was witness to what I later comprehended as national history. The summer of 1934 Mother and I drove from Seattle to visit Dad at his tent camp by the river, beneath McClellan Butte. That stretch of the Depression was eased for the Mannings by his job shoveling sand, gravel, and Portland cement into a concrete mixer, laying pavement eastward from North Bend. The history buff, poking around, comes upon artifacts of that era—concrete bridges whose dates are proudly inscribed by the builders, conscious as they were of the momentousness of what they were doing. A walk along dikes of the South Fork through North Bend passes bridges built for I-90, US 10, Sunset Highway, and both the Gilman and the Milwaukee Railways—a museum of transportation history, a century of bridge technology, the beginning of it closer to the youth of the Industrial Revolution than to our own time.

In 1940 the Floating Bridge across Lake Washington brought the Cascade Crest an hour closer to Seattle. During the months that Seattle was blacking out at night to baffle Japanese bombers, on a fine Sunday I took my sweetie on a Model A drive in the country—and out in the middle of nowhere was astounded to come upon an enormously wide swath of raw gravel. Nothing had been said about it in the press. It was a military secret, the eastern approach to the new bridge, to speed tanks and troops into Seattle to hurl the enemy back into Elliott Bay. At war's end I and a buddy fresh out of uniform dared a descent of cliffs to the bottom of snowmelt-thundering Snoqualmie Falls. A cloud of spray drifted over us—no, *not* spray, a significant portion of the very river itself. Clambering in the winter chill back up to the car, which had no heater, we stripped naked, giving the toll-taker at the Lake Washington bridge quite a start. Betty and I in our newlywed summer hiked to Snow Lake and camped. Driving back to Seattle we counted our cash and found only twenty cents, a nickel short of the toll. So we stopped in Issaquah for double-dip ice cream cones, a dime each, and drove home around the lake.

So much for personal history. When our view expands to the social history of our times, the family whose members saw to the creation of New York's Central Park emerges as a preserver on our side of the continent. The Olmsteds, while drawing plans for Seattle's parks and boulevards, cast their eyes beyond Lake Washington to a "string of pearls" extending from the New Rome on its Seven Hills to the Cascade Crest. Soon thereafter, a newborn legion of "tin-can tourists" began to aspire to national parks other than their backyard Rainier; an alternate name for the Sunset Highway was "Yellowstone Highway," the way from the Queen City to the geysers.

A principal if not the dominant theme of America in the first three-quarters of the twentieth century was "the freedom of the wheel." In the final quarter of the century, an obbligato began to make itself heard.

In 1975 Stan Unger, to publicize a proposal for a Sound-to-Mountains Trail, set out from Seattle's Discovery Park and walked 4 days on abandoned railroads, logging roads, and national forest trails, to be greeted at Snoqualmie Pass by his co-proposers with two cans of cold beer, one for internal consumption, one for his hot feet. Not government, not the press, not the Chamber of Commerce noticed. My 1978 book *Footsore 2* urged the establishment of a Cascade Gateway Recreation Area centered at North Bend; not even the North Bend Chamber of Commerce took note.

In 1981 President Reagan's Secretary of the Interior, James Watt, announced his plan to privatize public lands; a first step he proposed was to sell leases to prospect for geothermal energy in the Alpine Lakes Wilderness. The Conservation Division of The Mountaineers organized the Mountains-to-Sound March from Snoqualmie Pass to Seattle, led by Jim Whittaker, first American to climb Everest. The largest gathering of environmentalists in Northwest history cheered Jim and fellow marchers in to Gasworks Park, where they were addressed by two Congressmen and a row of other public officials. The march embarrassed everyone who had voted for Ronald Reagan and the affair was buried in the back pages, reporting Gasworks Park attendance at barely a third the number tallied by experienced crowd-counters. The time had not yet come.

It had in 1990, when a 5-day, 88-mile Mountains-to-Sound March was schemed, organized, and led by the Issaquah Alps Trails Club and Snoqualmie Valley Trails Club, the large group departing from Snoqualmie Pass on July 4 and arriving on July 8 at Seattle's Waterfront Park. Government, the press, and The Establishment noticed. In fact, several notables marched portions of the way or at least posed for TV cameras. In the fall of 1990 the Mountains-to-Sound Greenway Trust was incorporated. For a brochure published by the Trust for Public Lands, I borrowed the thinking if not the words of Thoreau and Olmsted: "The saving of the green spirit of Puget Sound City would be a model for elsewhere . . . a refuge within, a place to breathe deep and clean, to feel and think green peace, to re-create. A city operates at high pressure in close quarters—it's the hot steam of the boiler room that blasts out the great ideas that are civilization. However, too much heat boils the brains. Only by providing getaway space for a quick and easy cooling off can a city keep on cooking."

The Greenway concept requires rationalization of land management along the I-90 corridor. The public must rally around the Greenway standard to demand an end to unrestricted freedom of enterprise, must recognize that large tracts of forestlands, no more than Puget Sound rivers or the air or the sky, can be "private property" controlled by Adam Smith's "Invisible Hand," master of our economic system. A forest industry no longer tyrannized by the accountants' bottom line, and a nation needing the many products provided by forests, can be guaranteed a truly sustained yield of genuinely multiple uses, on the pattern set by Tiger Mountain State Forest.

Speaking for the pedestrian community, where all this began, in a press release for the 1990 march, I wrote: "The proposed Mountains-to-Sound Trail will lie in a Greenway corridor that will have room for every sort of recreational travel compatible with protection of the land, the water, the plants, the wildlife—and compatible with the nature-centered, non-kinetic, peace-and-quiet Greenway experience for which machine-burdened urbanites are crying. Last as well as first, the Greenway will serve as a 'habitat network' connecting wilderness of the Cascades to wild nooks within the urbanized core of Puget Sound City. In the phrase of Robinson Jeffers, a human society must be 'not man apart.'"

IRA'S PREFACE

Harvey and I met in July 1948 while climbing the Kautz Glacier of Mount Rainier. In fact we didn't actually meet because he took his rope team up one side of the icefall and I took mine up the other. We did meet later that year, in October, on the Nisqually Glacier, when I was photographing him for slides to illustrate the ice-climbing lecture in The Mountaineers' Climbing Course. We met often from then on, particularly when I was photograph advisor for *Mountaineering, The Freedom of the Hills,* the classic text that he and the Climbing Committee brought to press in 1960.

Our first close collaboration was in the same period, on a large-format photo book published in 1959, *High Worlds of the Mountain Climber;* three more photo books followed. When we got really thick, though, was in 1964, when the Literary Fund Committee that Harvey chaired came up with a scheme for a special kind of hiking guidebook, called on me for the photographs, and it just so happened that I had the same scheme cooking in my head. The Literary Fund Committee recruited an army of club members to contribute their experience. The text from many hands (and boots) was edited into a coherent unity by Harvey, the photos (and a lot of experience in getting them) were supplied by me. Thus, in 1966, was produced *100 Hikes in Western Washington.* That project served as a shakedown cruise for a continuing collaboration on a series of some ten hiking guides for Mountaineers Books.

Having worked with Harvey fifty years, I knew his dedication to preserving what he refers to as "the wildness without," by which he means the wildness outside the boundaries of urban civilization. I also had long since known his parallel concern for "the wildness within," which is to say the nooks enclosed by civilization. He had expressed this concern in his (and, photographically, my) guidebooks to walking the beaches and the lowlands and foothills.

Reading the manuscript for this book, I learned about still another Harvey. I had no concept of his vision of the urban wildland or of the years Harvey spent exploring the area from Cougar Mountain to Snoqualmie Pass and how he provided the inspiration and leadership to change a vision of an urban wildland into a reality. Harvey did not do it alone, but with a dedicated team of workers who were backed up by thousands of hikers who had become green-bonded on trails found in our other guidebooks.

Only an hour's drive from Seattle, Snoqualmie Pass is popular with hikers. On a single good summer day some 4,000 overwhelm the trails leading into the Alpine Lakes Wilderness. In a year 25,000 hike the Snow LakeTrail; 18,000 the Pratt Lake–Granite Mountain trails; 10,000 the Pacific Crest Trail; 18,000 the Denny Creek trail; 4,000 the Mason Lake trail; and 10,000 the Talapus Lake trail.

Mason Lake from Bandera Mountain (Hike 25)

Outside this designated wilderness, 15,000 a year visit Annette Lake; 10,000 McClellan Butte; and 50,000 Mount Si. Two other trails on state land climb to views on Dirty Harry's Peak and Mailbox Peak; these are unsigned and parking is a problem and so are less used.

To preserve the wildness of the wilderness, more alternative trails are needed. There is a large potential for non-wilderness trails on forest and state lands in the I-90 corridor that could provide more opportunities for pedestrians, equestrians, and bikers.

THE USER FEE DEBATE

Now, there's this new thing called the Northwest Forest Pass. The Forest Service sells it and warns that if you don't display it on your car at a trailhead, you will suffer. Rangers will frown at you, issue tickets, which may be warnings, or they may demand you pay the judge a good deal more than the cost of the pass. Volunteer enforcers wearing hardhats as haloes will call down upon you the vengeance of Heaven, point fingers, and cry "Shame! Shame!"

However, environmental organizations have with few exceptions denounced the pass as a plot to put the Forest Service in the business of "industrial wreckreation." Indeed, active citizen support comes mainly from organizations that promote use of motorcycles and sports utility vehicles and snowmobiles. It is true enough that the Forest Service is scandalously underfunded by Congress. That is the problem, as well as the proper place to go for funds to preserve trails.

In summary, there is organized resistance to the pass, with many individuals urging the course of Henry David Thoreau, who went to jail rather than pay a tax imposed to fund the invasion of Mexico. At this stage of a conflict that is only just getting intense, it is up to each and every hiker to make up his or her mind. At the least, every hiker ought to write his or her congresspeople angry letters. Enough letters and this exhortation can be deleted from the next edition of this book.

—Harvey Manning
December 2000

The Northwest Forest Pass has made me feel as if I am standing by myself in the middle of a buffalo stampede while Harvey and everyone else is rushing by me to condemn the user fee. Harvey and many other environmentalists see the forest pass as a slippery slope leading to all kinds of industrial recreation. I see the forest pass as the best defense against industrial recreation.

We do not pay to enjoy the forest. Your Northwest Forest Pass helps pay for the facilities we use (campgrounds, parking areas, trails, etc.). The use of the forest itself is free, but like the church, we are asked to contribute to the maintenance of its facilities.

The annual Northwest Forest Pass is free to volunteers who spend two days on trail maintenance. I spent this summer exploring seldom-used trails. For all the days on the trail, I only parked twice at a trailhead requiring a pass. No pass is needed to park near the abandoned trails I enjoy. I do not mind climbing over or under logs or plowing through brush, and I love the solitude on these rarely used trails. The only cost is the $5.00 for gas to drive to the trailhead, and the labor of mending clothes torn by the brush. According to a state survey, there are one million hikers in this state. One hiker has very little impact on a trail, but since the Snow Lake Trail was reconstructed in 1990, over two million feet (that's twenty-five thousand hikers a year) have worn the cliff section of the Snow Lake Trail to nothing by sharp blasted rocks. Donating hundreds of hours, volunteers have kept the rest of the trail in good shape.

Harvey and I completely agree with the problem of industrial recreation of our public lands. Harvey's term "industrial wreckreation" fits perfectly. MONEY TALKS. Money talked in the 1800s when Congress gave the railroads their checkerboard of timberland. Money talked in the 1920s when "Mine to Market Roads" were built to help miners find the "Mother Lode." Money talked when logging roads gobbled up hundreds of miles of trail. Money talked (and is still talking) when the Forest Service turned over a thousand miles of trail to motorcycles. Money talks when snowmobiles displace cross-country skiers. Money, lots of money, is buying permits to build destination resorts on the edge of wilderness areas. These resorts will have daily horse trips and turn trail tread to gravel, making the trails miserable for hikers. There will be sightseeing helicopters that may drop tourists off for an hour-long picnic by a pristine lake or a flower-covered ridge top.

Until now there has been no money to speak for the hiker.

What Congress has given us, Congress can take away, including our wilderness areas. It is important that people have decent trails to experience for themselves the forest, wildlife, clean water, flower-covered meadows, and glaciers. This experience enables people to become green-bonded and motivates them to form a large constituency that will support and preserve our wildlands from "industrial wreakreation."

Up to this point, Harvey and I are together. Our solutions, however, are 180 degrees apart. Harvey and other environmentalists have good reasons to believe Congress should subsidize our trails as they did in the 1980s. However, I have given up on Congress, for eastern members I have talked to see no reason to subsidize western trails: If volunteers can maintain the Appalachian Trail, we westerners can maintain our trails.

Thanks to the money equivalent created by thousands of volunteer hours and money from your Northwest Forest Pass, hikers finally have **money that talks,** money that officials and land managers will listen to.

—Ira Spring
December 2000

THE MOUSE THAT IS LEARNING TO ROAR, OR GREEN-BONDING FOR A GREEN FUTURE

Great wilderness has many attributes: spectacular views, flower fields and meadows, lakes and streams, ancient or at least virgin forest, animals and birds, solitude, silence—escape from sounds of motors, a chance to hear birds, wind, and sometimes true silence—and a primitive experience with a physical and mental challenge. Seldom does one find all these on one trail or even in one wilderness. But most of us find a quality wilderness experience with just two or three of these attributes. For a family we met on the Pyramid Lake trail (North Cascades National Park), their hike was an experience of a lifetime, even though the trail has just one of those attributes. Again, at Mount Rainier, we were on our way down the Rampart Ridge trail when we were stopped by a couple who just had to tell someone about their wonderful experience, even though they saw only forest and were considerably challanged physically by this, their first step in their "green-bonding." "Bonding" is the term for the ties developed by an offspring to a parent—a newborn baby to its mother, a newborn fawn to its doe. "Green-bonding" describes the emotional ties a person develops to the great out-of-doors while hiking trails, enjoying the fresh air of wildlands and the flowers, trees, wildlife, and surrounding natural beauty.

Green-bonding also results in green supporters—a constituency whose responsibility it is to care for its wildlands, working as advocates by lobbying for its protection and safekeeping. Thousands of such green-bonded people wrote to their congresspeople urging passage of the 1984 Washington Wilderness Act to protect Washington wilderness from deforestation and development. Their pleas were heard by our Congressional delegates, and 1,000,000 acres were added to our state's dedicated wilderness. During Forest Management Planning by the U.S. Forest Service, 10,000 green-bonded people wrote the Mount Baker–Snoqualmie National Forest stressing the importance of trails, and the managers took steps to preserve trails. Often the only barrier between a wilderness area and its destruction is the thickness of a single sheet of paper—your letter.

However, there is bonding to things other than green—to decent homes, to good schools, to safe streets and highways, to convenient shopping malls, to pleasure domes for athletic contests. As the nation continues a population growth that entails more wooden houses, more factories, more vacation retreats near national parks, more helicopter pads, more space-consumptive toys, the result is a massive de-greening by money-bonded entrepreneurs who efficiently organize and heavily fund a nigh-religious crusade to despoil the public green for private profit. For the last five years Congress has entertained serious proposals to decommission "surplus" park and wilderness land and hand it over to the "private sector." Fortunately, in 1996 there were enough green-bonded people in the nation to halt the giveaway with their letters. But further raids must be expected. Will there be enough green-bonded people in the year 2005 or 2010 to protect public lands?

The money-bonding of commercial-industrial entrepreneurs is the heart of the matter, is the essence of our economy. It cannot be kept in check simply by our taking a hike. However, with lots of green-bonded support it can be redirected. By our feet. That's what this book is for—to mobilize feet. Prior to World War II, the White Chuck River country had many trails but few hikers—too few to prevent a postwar logging road from climbing the valley nearly to Kennedy Hot Springs, converting a many-day backpack to an afternoon stroll. We had the Golden Horn all to ourselves, but because there was no trail, few had been there and no constituency existed large enough to obtain it for the North Cascades National Park. The Ragged Ridge, Eagle Rock, and the huge flower fields of the Jackman Creek roadless area had no trails, so therefore no constituency sufficient to obtain 1984 designation as wilderness—and since these areas still have no trails they may lack enough green-bonded support for the next go-around.

There were abundant trails on the motor-infested Dark Divide, Mad River, and Golden Lakes trails, but hikers too disgusted with the noise and speed of motorcycles that utilized these "multi-use" areas avoided these gems, leaving too few voices to make the case for including the trails in the Washington Wilderness Act. In the 1950s the trail from Snoqualmie Pass to Snow Lake was hiked by 800 people a year. The annual number now is 25,000! The backcountry was uncrowded back then; that was the good news. The bad news outweighs the good—there wasn't enough green-bonded public support to prevent logging roads from gobbling up thousands of miles of trails or to stop motorcycles from running us off many of our pedestrian favorites.

Pedestrians are the most numerous recreationists, by far, in Washington State. A 1988 survey by the state Interagency for Outdoor Recreation counted in excess of 1,000,000 people, old and young, who walk all sorts of trails, short and long, urban and wildland. They average four day-hikes a year; almost 500,000 (or half of them) backpack at least once a year. Yet these 1,000,000-plus hikers are led around by 41,300 wheelers, that being the number of off-road vehicle registrations issued by the state Department of Licensing. The Forest Service has set aside 980 miles of our trails for 41,300 motorcyclists, but only 1,460 miles for the 1,000,000 hikers in this state.

Unfortunately, only a couple thousand of those 1,000,000 hikers belong to an organization that will keep them informed of trail use, leaving 998,000 hikers unaware of the overall picture of what may happen to trails without their support. Most new hikers walk the trails with one or two friends, seeing no reason to join a hiking club. But outdoor organizations serve as information gatherers, to direct your letter traffic to the appropriate officials, to save your wildlands.

What good could one letter do? Well, one letter to the Okanogan–Wenatchee National Forest, added to 4,999 others, convinced a federal judge to return the North Fork Entiat to non-motorized use. One plus one, plus some more ones—that adds up to green power. We have been told by Forest Service employees of occasions, during meetings in which land use was being considered, when just one letter has turned a decision. If that letter came from a green-bonded friend, great! If it was from a motorcyclist, yuck! But we have no one but ourselves to blame.

WRITE LETTERS

To supervisors of National Forests (for addresses see the end of this section). Motorcycles make more noise than feet, but letters can silence the roar, can penetrate the minds and souls of officials.

To government officials—congresspeople, senators, the president, not forgetting, in appropriate cases, state legislators and governors.

To newspapers. Editors welcome letters that have news value, which is to say, really-true information. (But if you don't have fresh information, venting a bit of old-fashioned emotion can't hurt.)

That's what we need. More letters. (Write them!) More well-informed hikers. (Join a group!) More green power. (Flex your muscles!)

USE YOUR FEET

Harvey points out that your feet bones are connected to your leg bones, leg bones to the hip bones, hip bones to the backbone, backbone to the head bone, head bone to the letter-writing finger bones. Your feet know the land better than do the heads of public officials. Insert into those heads the knowledge your feet have learned by taking one step at a time at a respectful, studious pace. Keep your feet at their studies of the wildlands—your land, with your obligation to be its steward and advocate. Join a group (or two) dedicated to preserving foot trails. Read the bulletins they publish covering current wildland issues.

When they sound the danger siren, hop to it! Get those letters in the mail! So write. And get cracking!

—Ira Spring

Following are organizations that are strenuously working to preserve trail country. Join one (or more). Read their publications, which alert you to dangers to trails and tell you who needs to get your letters.

ALPS (Alpine Lakes Protection
Society)
100 9th Avenue, E-6
Bellevue, WA 98004-5401

North Cascades Conservation
Council
P.O. Box 95980
Seattle, WA 98145-1980

The Cascadians
P.O. Box 2201
Yakima, WA 99908

Sierra Club, Cascade Chapter
8511 15th Avenue NE, Room 201
Seattle, WA 98155

Intermountain Alpine Club
P.O. Box 505
Richland, WA 99352-1990

Snoqualmie Valley Trails Club
P.O. Box 1741
North Bend, WA 97202

Issaquah Alps Trails Club (IATC)
P.O. Box 122
Issaquah, WA 98027

Spokane Mountaineers
P.O. Box 1013
Spokane, WA 99208

Mazamas
909 NW 19th Avenue
Portland, OR 97302

Washington Alpine Club
P.O. Box 352
Seattle, WA 98111

Mid-FORC (Middle Fork Outdoor
Recreation Coalition)
P.O. Box 25809
Seattle, WA 98125

Washington Trails Association
1305 Fourth Avenue, Room 512
Seattle, WA 98101

Washington Wilderness Coalition
4649 Sunnyside N
Seattle, WA 98103

The Mountaineers
300 Third Avenue West
Seattle, WA 98119
    The Mountaineers has branches in Tacoma, Everett, Olympia, Wenatchee, and Bellingham.

Magazines carrying trail reports:

Pack and Paddle
P.O. Box 1063
Port Orchard, WA 98366

Signpost Magazine
Published by the Washington
Trails Association

INTRODUCTION

On every hike where a shout for help might not bring quick assistance to the lost or injured or ill, each person—and every person—must carry the Ten Essentials. In recent years, as the list has been so tiresomely dinned into us by the media, it has been smirked at by disciples of Ed Abbey (of whom I am one), who said, "Americans have too much stuff. They carry too much of it in the wilderness. Personally, I like to give Nature a fair crack at me." Let the smirkers take note that the list was drawn up by leaders of the Climbing Course (of whom I was one), sitting in committee in a time of sorrow, determining what missing equipment would have saved the lives of friends now forever missing.

THE TEN ESSENTIALS
1. Extra clothing—enough so that if a sunny-warm morning yields to a rainy-windy afternoon, or if an accident keeps the party out overnight, hypothermia ("exposure" or "freezing to death") will not be a threat
2. Extra food—enough so that something is left over at the planned end of the trip, in case the actual end is the next day
3. Sunglasses—if travel on snow for more than a few minutes may be involved
4. Knife—for first aid and emergency firebuilding (making kindling)
5. Firestarter—a candle or chemical fuel for starting a fire with wet wood
6. First-aid kit—and the knowledge to use it
7. Matches—in a waterproof container
8. Flashlight—with extra bulb and batteries
9. Map—topographical maps (maps in this book are impressionistic and not acceptable for precise navigation)
10. Compass—and the knowledge to use it

Beyond that, while gearing and garbing up, keep ever in mind the wisdom of Abbey, prophet of the dawning Age of Minimalism. My own basic training came at Camp Parsons, where, after the hike party was ready for the trail, the leader would make everybody spread their gear on the ground and would then go about kicking aside the sweaters and raincoats and mufflers and teddy bears Mother had sent along to camp. On a 5-day, 70-mile running of the ridges, a Boy Scout hardly ever froze or starved to death, nor died of thirst so long as he saved a prune pit from breakfast. Still at bottom a hungry, thirsty, shivering Parsons Minimalist in the tradition of John Muir (asked how he prepared for a trip in the wilds, he said, "I take a half-pound of tea and a loaf of bread and climb over the back fence"), I'm uneasy about counseling an age up to its eyebrows in credit cards and Stuff; I relied for wisdom on the pundits of REI in the book I wrote for them, *Backpacking: One Step at a Time*. It was a bestseller from first publication in 1972, rated the top of the heap by the *Boy Scout Handbook, Ms. Magazine,* the *John Birch Society Journal,* and the *NBC Morning Show.* Hardly any of the equipment in its pages is on today's market. Many metals now in use weren't invented when Jim Whittaker was the first American to climb Everest. Many popular fabrics only just yesterday came out of the chemist's pot. Prices are orders of magnitude higher.

However, its attitude is, in my opinion, still valid. In the Depression one heard (hunger) "Brother, can you spare a dime?" and (bitter irony) "I wonder what the poor people are doing today?" Social historians have observed that the Depression generation (mine) is psychically crippled, unfit for the age of software dot com. Through the swirl of high-tech high fashion, we wander in a daze, asking, "Who's hoeing the potatoes?"

Licorice Fern Wall on Cougar Mountain (Hike 1)

INFORMATION SUMMARIES

For each trip we have provided a data summary that permits a person with a little trail experience to determine if a hike suits his/her energy and ambition.

Our "allow xx hours" must be used with a personal conversion factor. The figures here are based roughly on doing about 1½ miles an hour on the flat, and/or gaining about 700 feet of elevation an hour. A person in good condition can, of course, do much better and have the satisfaction of sneering at the fuddy-duddy guidebook. Let me warn that there are guidebooks whose authors guard their egos against sneers by giving times that would win the Olympic Games—this is known as guidebook-author bragging. You won't find me bragging about the morning I did Mount Si in 1½ hours from the coffee shop in North Bend. I thought I was being pursued.

The "high point" entry tells you much about the vegetation and views to expect, and especially about the amount of snow at that place in any given month.

The intent of the month(s) listed is to tell when, in an average normal year (whatever that is), a trail is probably sufficiently snowfree for pleasure walking, meaning less than a foot of snow or only occasional deeper patches. Several factors are involved. One is elevation. Another is distance from Puget Sound, whose large volume of above-freezing water warms winter air masses. In any locality, higher is generally snowier, but also, for identical elevations the farther from saltwater is generally snowier. And mountain valleys, acting like giant iceboxes, generally are snowier than nearby west slopes, which get as much snow as north and east ones but also get more sun (and also more sun than valley flats) and thus melt out faster.

The "closer is better" rule says a destination 10 miles from a person's home is 100 times (geographers have found the increase to be geometric rather than arithmetic) less attractive than one of equal merit across the street. The closeness of the Greenway to the core of Puget Sound City is such that the number of feet on trails of the I-90 corridor has been growing not geometrically but exponentially.

Building new trails? Rationing use of existing ones? Limiting the number of hikers per day? Eliminating certain uses as incompatible with preservation of "the resource" (that is, the soils, the plants, the water, the wildlife) and/or with providing a "wildland experience"? Balancing restrictions against the opportunity for "green-bonding"? Requiring permits, as was routine ("fire permits") when Ira and I were hot stuff on the trails? Charging fees to help pay for increased costs of trail maintenance, new trail construction, more wilderness rangers to protect "the resource" and to keep us honest?

Questions, questions, questions. Check at the information desk you'll find in any sizable backpacking shop, and call the U.S. Forest Service–National Park Service Information Center in Seattle, Washington, at (206) 470-4060.

COURTESY AND CONSIDERATION

If you can carry it in full, you certainly are able to carry it out empty. *Pack it out!* Every can, foil wrap, and orange peel. *Leave no trace.*

Where privies are provided, use them. Where not, the ethical behavior on crowded trails—and certain to become, in time, the legal requirement—is to double-bag your solid wastes and *pack them out.* The older rule, not yet obsolete everywhere, is: Eliminate wastes in spots well removed from watercourses. Dig a shallow hole in the "biological disposer layer" (typically about 6 inches), then touch a match to the toilet paper—*but not in forest fire season!* Fussy old people have called t.p. "the 11th essential." It is no such thing. Rare is the wildland acreage lacking suitable leaves. Higher up, snow is very effective and refreshing. Finally, cover the evidence with biological disposer soil.

Yes indeed, "closer is better," but as a corollary on the I-90 Corridor, "you gotta take the bitter with the better." As Colonel Custer said that day

West Tiger 3 (Hike 3)

in Montana, "Where in tarnation did all these Indians come from?" They, of course, meanwhile were asking where all those dang bluecoats came from. It is not necessary for every I-90 hike to replay Little Big Horn but, sorry to say, there are people who feel that being in wildlands gives them the right—nay, the duty—to act like wildmen. What was socially acceptable for Ira and me, roistering through the empty (except for Boy Scouts) Olympics of the 1930s does not amuse the huddled masses on the Snow Lake Trail of the 1990s.

On the trail, when footsteps approach from the rear, stand aside and smile them by. When you approach from the rear, if your footsteps seem not to be heard, politely clear your throat, ask "May I pass?" and smile on by. On popular trails, running is only tolerable if the runner slows to nearly the walker's speed to pass and only resumes the *thud-thud* and *huff-puff* when well past.

WATER

Don't sell the prune pits short. However, for day hikes fill your bottles at home, toss a couple cans of pop or juice in the rucksack, and that takes care of that.

Ira and I grew up taking care to avoid drinking from slimy puddles that might cause the "Boy Scout trots." In the 1970s an outbreak of "beaver fever" devastated newcomers to the wilds. The culprit was identified as *Giardia,* a parasite that spends part of its life swimming and part in the intestinal tracts of wildlife, dogs, and people.

Giardiasis is regularly contracted from the public water systems of the entire Third World, many of the Second, and not a few of America, including some in foothills of the Cascades; it can also be contracted from fresh fruits and vegetables in Seattle supermarkets and salad bars of popular restaurants. Most humans feel no ill effects (but may become carriers), others have symptoms that may include temporarily crippling diarrhea; the treatment is nearly as unpleasant. The reason giardiasis has become "epidemic" is that today there are more people in the backcountry, more people drinking water contaminated by animals, and more people contaminating the water.

On day hikes, when your water bottle from home is empty, you are unlikely to have a stove in your rucksack with which to boil water 10 minutes, a treatment 100 percent effective against not only *Giardia* but the myriad other filthy little blighters that may upset your digestion or—as with some forms of hepatitis—destroy your liver. Therefore always carry one of several iodine treatments such as Potable Aqua or the more complicated method that employs iodine crystals.

CRIME

During the Depression, thieves could have plundered a whole Boy Scout troop and lost money on the deal. The same was true of stealing from the

Khaki Gang after WW II. Mountain Trooper boots went for $2.50, ski troop "mook" parkas for a buck, Navy foulweather parkas were two bits, which also was the going price for Bergen packs, wool trousers, wool sweaters, watch caps, mittens (with holes for the trigger finger), and Air Corps "raccoon" goggles. Just about everything else was a nickel or a dime, including khaki handkerchiefs. As for a 7x11-foot life-raft sail, you had a hard time finding those for less than $5.00, and feather-down sleeping bags, the inner and outer, were bid up early on to $10.00 the pair. Strip a climber to the skin and he'd lose no more than a couple of days' pay, and where was the fence who wouldn't laugh in the robber's face?

Cut to the 1990s. The cars parked at trailheads along I-90, and their contents left inside while the owners are walking, have a value approaching the GNP of a Third World nation. I-90 is the regular workplace of our own American Third World. Locking the car just invites smashed windows. Your clever hiding places are the first places the experts look. A team of skilled professionals can case, can-open, and high-grade a row of cars while hikers gape open-mouthed, and be back on the freeway and miles away before the jaws close.

So keep your Beamer in the garage at home, drive to the trailhead in a beater, and leave nothing in it but dirty socks and empty root beer cans.

SAFETY CONSIDERATIONS

Inclusion of a trail in this book does not mean it will be safe for you. The route may have changed since the description herein was written. Creeks flood. Gravity pulls down trees and rocks. Brush grows up. The weather changes from season to season, day to day, hour to hour. Wind blows, rain soaks, lightning strikes, the sun sets, temperature drops, snow falls, avalanches happen.

A guidebook cannot guarantee you are safe for the trail. You vary from decade to decade, year to year, day to day, morning to afternoon to dark and stormy night.

You can reduce backcountry risks by being informed, equipped, and alert; by recognizing hazards and knowing and respecting your limits. However, you cannot eliminate risk, and neither can the attorney hired by your next of kin. It's a dangerous world out there. Perhaps you'd be happier as an armchair adventurer—but even there you may want to strap yourself in as a precaution against earthquakes.

KEY TO MAP SYMBOLS

═══════	freeway		643	trail number
+++++++	railroad		℗	parking for hike start
▬▬▬▬	paved road		♦	ranger station
══════	gravel or dirt road		⌂	building
========	primitive (walking) road		∷	buildings in town
------------	trail described in text		▲	campground
- - - - - - -	trail not described in text		开	picnic area
·················	cross-country route described in text		▰	shelter
·················	cross-country route not described in text		◭	backcountry campsite
· — · — · —	boundary (park or wilderness area)		☗	lookout
· — · — · —	powerline		✗	mine
•——————•	ski lift		) (	pass
84	interstate highway		] [	bridge
97	US highway		•—•	gate
530	state highway		∿	river or stream
26	county highway		∿₊₊	waterfall
3060	National Forest road		▬	lake
			marsh	marsh
			glacier	glacier

Squak Mountain trail (Hike 2)

ISSAQUAH ALPS

The Old Mountains stretched from the Yakima area to Cape Flattery. The Cascades rose up to swallow them at one end, the Olympics at the other. The Puget Lobe of the Cordilleran Ice Sheet rode over their summits. Two remnants survive. The Kitsap Peninsula is dominated by the Blue Mountains; Bremerton is built on their foothills. The "Seven Hills of the New Rome" are foothills of the other, which reaches 20-odd miles from Lake Washington, through suburbs and exurbs, to the Cascade front.

This second remnant of "old" peaks never had a name until 1976, when they became the Issaquah Alps. They became so because I said so. For a quarter century I'd been living there, walking there, reveling in the immensity of wildland just out my back door. And my front door, too. But as the years passed, in looking down to the lowlands beneath my heights, I witnessed the unrelenting sprawl of Puget Sound City, an ocean of houses and shopping centers, freeways and arterials creeping steadily nearer the base of our Old Mountains, lapping at our greenwoods, preparing to climb through them, drown them.

A window of social opportunity remained open, yet soon would snap shut. Something would have to be done, quick. What? I'd no idea. But I did hearken to Linnaeus, deviser of the binomial system for naming plants, who said that unless you know the name of a thing, you lose your knowledge of it. Before anything could be done to preserve wildness in this anomalous geography, it had to have a name. Quick was the word, and quick is what we were. In a half-dozen years the Issaquah Alps Trails Club, and the environmentalists for which it was the coalition spearhead, succeeded in preserving hundreds of miles of walking trails. More significantly (and the whole point of the crusade for trails), their existence and use by a large constituency of pedestrians and equestrians resulted in thousands of acres of wildland ecosystems and wildlife habitat being saved from the single-use (money, money, money) categorical imperative of Adam Smith's "Invisible Hand"—the free market. The system of footpaths now provides the overwhelming majority of guaranteed wheelfree walking opportunities within an automobile half-hour of homes in King County and northern Pierce and southern Snohomish Counties, and from ferries from Kitsap County. Photographs from the air—indeed, from outer space—show a startlingly enormous green space *within* Puget Sound City. Amazing, but true.

To be sadly sure, as the new millennium begins it will be the rare automobile anywhere that can count on so much as getting out of its home driveway in a half-hour. Among the possible solutions to gridlock are (1) a runaway asteroid or comet, such as is hypothesized to have abruptly terminated the age of the dinosaurs; (2) a pandemic on the order of the Great Pestilence of the fourteenth century; (3) deliberately phasing out unrestricted use of the private automobile in favor of assorted systems of public transit. A preference for alternative (3) was the reason we Issaquah Alpinists, in staging the 1977 mass ascent of West Tiger Mountain from a trailhead at the bus stop in downtown Issaquah, publicized it as a pilgrimage to "Wilderness on the Metro 210."

Tradition Lake, Tiger Mountain State Forest (Hike 3)

Westernmost of the Issaquah Alps is Cougar Mountain, 1595 feet—an elevation as great as three and a half Queen Anne Hills piled one atop the other. In 1985 the Cougar Mountain Regional Wildland Park was dedicated; the park nucleus and adjoining green and quiet spaces total nearly 8 square miles free from the noise of internal combustion engines, and free from the harassing speed of wheels, whether four to a vehicle or two. Neither the press nor the chambers of commercers have awakened to boast that this is the largest urban wildland in the United States.

Next east is Squak Mountain, 2000 feet. In 1972 the Bullitt family, earlier having bought 590 acres of the summit ridge as a private retreat, gave the land to Washington State Parks, the deed of gift stipulating that there were to be no buildings, no tree-cutting, no bulldozing, no roads, no machines, no wheels. In 1989 and years following, state and county and city of Issaquah combined resources to enlarge the protected area to nearly 5 square miles, the whole of it dedicated (by the Bullitts) as a "natural area."

The centerpiece of the Alps, Tiger Mountain, is not a single peak but a whole range: West Tiger, jutting out in the sky over Issaquah and I-90; Middle Tiger, above the Issaquah-Hobart Road; South Tiger, above Highway 18, and the highest, East Tiger, 3004 feet, rising nearly that many feet above I-90, Highway 18, and the Raging River. The 1981 establishment of the 13,500-acre Tiger Mountain State Forest brought all three of the "core" Alps into the plan of the Cosmic Architect as revealed to and by the Issaquah Alps Trails Club.

These astounding victories of the environmental coalition, unparalleled in the history of our region, testify to the wisdom that lurks in the spirits of citizens and can be brought bursting forth when they hear the Word of the Architect preached by street-corner friars. However, lest one be amazed that not all the Puget Sound country has similarly been preserved as a "green and pleasant land," the sobering reality is that the triumph in the Alps was built on pure dumb luck. Yes, the window was open. Yes, the friars were lusty. Nevertheless, the opportunity would have been blocked by the Establishment's bottom line had it not been for three fortuities.

First came the Bullitt family's gift on Squak. Ironically, State Parks was reluctant. Where, they asked, can our rangers drive their trucks? Where can we park the Winnebagoes? How do we flush toilets? The response of the Bullitts was that you don't, not in *our* Natural Area. The Squak gift was ultimately accepted by State Parks but was then ignored. The Bullitts considered revoking the gift and seeking some better guardian—perhaps even the Issaquah Alps Trails Club! Eventually State Parks shouldered the responsibilities spelled out in the deed of gift; long before that, though, the existence of the wildland, neglected though it was for years, stood as an inspiration to street-corner preachers of the Word of the Architect.

Second and third came two political victories, one in King County, the other in the state, both upsets so shocking that there was an epidemic of developers falling off their bar stools.

Randy Revelle was not given the chance of a snowflake in Florida in his 1981 challenge of the incumbent King County Executive, the developers' handyman. A campaign press conference atop Cougar Mountain at which he pledged to get the park created was dismissed by the wise money as the quixotic idiosyncrasy of a loser. His emergence as a winner set off a panic in the County Courthouse, a rabble of "fixers" scrambling through the corridors trying to wiggle their way into the Democratic Party. To the rescue of the Republican Party's bottom line came a developer from California who bought the Seattle baseball team, threatened to move the franchise out of town, blamed Randy Revelle as a bad sport, and so terrified the sportswriters that they whipped the fans into a hysterical bloc vote which, when added to the kneejerk of the bottom-liners, replaced Revelle with a free-marketeer, Executive Zero (nobody ever can remember his name). However, before leaving office Revelle in 1985 presided over the dedication of Cougar Mountain Regional Wildland Park.

Nobody had heard of Brian Boyle before 1980, when he came out of nowhere and toppled Ol' King Cole from the throne of State Land Commissioner he had occupied since the Pleistocene. Boyle took a hike on Tiger Mountain with leaders of the Issaquah Alps Trails Club and listened to their concept of an "urban tree farm" that would give industry an assured and stable base as the city grew up all around and that would manage all resources of the forest for *true* multiple use and for a *true* sustained yield. As head of the Department of Natural Resources (DNR), he engineered the land exchange that locked up most of Tiger in public ownership and in 1981 established the 13,500-acre Tiger Mountain State Forest as "a working forest in an urban environment." A citizens advisory committee spent nearly two years with DNR staff studying the mountain, concluding that the northern sector was of greater and more sustainable value for other purposes than timber production; thus, in 1989, the DNR shepherded through the state Legislature a measure that designated this sector as the West Tiger Mountain Natural Resources Conservation Area, to be managed under regulations that echo the National Wilderness Act of 1964.

South of Tiger, beyond Highway 18, is Taylor Mountain, of which 1700 acres were purchased in 1998 for a King County Forest. North of Tiger, beyond I-90, is Grand Ridge, where the state and county have acquired substantial tracts for open space. Hiking can be done now on these public lands but the trail plans are in progress; guidebooking is premature.

In my *Footsore 2* of 1978 (now out of print), I lobbied hard for Rattlesnake Mountain and explored the most of it. In 1990 the "Rattlesnake Rangers" of the Issaquah and Snoqualmie Valley Trails Clubs hooked my routes together in a splendid system, described in my 1993 *Hiking the Mountains-to-Sound Greenway* (also out of print now). The 1994 creation of a 2000-acre Rattlesnake Mountain Scenic Area jointly managed by the state DNR and King County Parks as a Natural Resources Conservation Area has delayed regularization of the volunteer-whacked paths, which must await completion and implementation of a management plan. Nevertheless, my personal favorite since my first ascent of it in 1952, Rattlesnake Ledge, is open for business.

Now, if Rattlesnake is the eastern terminus of the Issaquah Alps, and Mt. Washington the front of the Cascades, what does that make Cedar Butte? In these pages we make it an Honorary Alp.

Two rivers course through the Issaquah Alps. The Raging River heads on Rattlesnake, drains Taylor and Tiger and Grand Ridge in passing, and empties into the Snoqualmie at Fall City. The citizens of Preston and Upper Preston are leading a plan for parks and trails in the river vicinity.

From Taylor Mountain to Rattlesnake Mountain, the boundary of the Issaquah Alps is the Cedar River Watershed. You can't go walking there, or hunting or picnicking or horsing around. You can't go there at all—and you shouldn't want to. The 143 square miles of the river's drainage basin supply 12 million residents of Puget Sound City with 108 million gallons a day of the purest water any big city could wish. The advocates of multiple use argue the watershed could be opened to public pleasuring while maintaining the purity. However, water purity is only one argument against public recreation in the watershed. Of equal importance is its role as refuge safeguarding *the largest wildlife population so close to any major city of the planet.*

Just about every animal native to the region is resident—elk (more than 600), black bears, bobcats, lynx, some 15 resident cougars, as many deer as these cats need for lunch, a few mountain goats, a host of coyotes, and skunks-porcupines-weasels-raccoons-beavers-aplodontia-moles-voles-shrews-mice. They move freely out of the watershed sanctuary to Rattlesnake and Taylor, thence to Tiger, Squak, and Cougar, and from there into outer neighborhoods of Puget Sound City.

Of six pairs of common loons known to nest in Washington in 1989, three were in the watershed, and an osprey pair as well. Harlequin ducks, common mergansers, swans, and other waterfowl nest here in winter, as do a circus of raptors and corvids and dickybirds. The ancient forests are home to spotted, great horned, and pygmy owls, as well as pileated and hairy and downy woodpeckers, and the waters to sandpipers and dippers. Golden eagles patrol the ridges and bald eagles scavenge the streambanks. Tailed frogs and Pacific giant salamanders hop and slither. Bats fly by night, butterflies in summer sun.

To a society that increasingly prizes wildlife habitat in close proximity to people habitat, the Cedar River Watershed is a treasure house. At least one mountain sheep has been sighted. Wolves have been reported. Someday the grizzly may be allowed to return.

The public is not totally excluded. Hikers can look down into the Cedar from trails on Taylor, Rattlesnake, Cedar Butte, Washington, and McClellan Butte. Other watershed-edge sites may accommodate trails in future. You can look all you want, but you mustn't touch.

1 COUGAR MOUNTAIN REGIONAL WILDLAND PARK: WILDSIDE TRAIL–RED TOWN TRAIL

Loop trip: 2 miles
Hiking time: Allow 1½ hours
High point: 750 feet
Elevation gain: 200 feet
Hikable: All year
Maps: Issaquah Alps Trails Club *Trails of Cougar Mountain;* Green Trails No. 2035, Cougar Mountain, Squak Mountain

The master plan adopted by the King County Council in 1994 specifies low-impact, non-mechanized recreation in Cougar Mountain Regional Wildland Park. In America's largest in-city wildland park, the slow have the right-of-way; there is absolute freedom from wheeled speed.

The Issaquah Alps Trails Club publishes a comprehensive guide and map to the park's nearly 100 miles of walking. Here I merely whet the appetite with a saunter that can entertain an easy morning or afternoon or summer evening, but can also serve as overture to full days of energetic ambling.

Go off I-90 at Exit 13 to Lakemont Boulevard SE. Drive over The Pass

De Leo Wall

and descend to Coal Creek Townsite (Red Town Trailhead), elevation 640 feet. Across the county road from this trailhead is another, in Coal Creek Wildland Park, where the Coal Creek trail follows the route of Seattle's first railroad, the Seattle & Walla Walla. The history is thick here. The buff will want to carry another book from the Issaquah Alps Trails Club, *Coals of Newcastle*, by Lucile and Dick McDonald.

At the bulletin board just inside the Red Town gate, pick up a (free) trail map. Begin your initiation saunter on the Wildside Trail, cross the pretty bridge over Coal Creek, thread through the mysterious heaps of waste rock dumped by the gypo miners who scavenged the seams after the Pacific Coast Coal Company left in 1930.

Turn left on the Rainbow Town trail to the Ford Slope, the mine entry from 1914 to 1926. A bit beyond, turn right on the trail to the site of the sawmill that cut mine timbers. The mill pond (which doubled as the Ol' Swimmin' Hole) was sedimented in by a 1980s flood. Ascend the valley wall to rejoin the Wildside Trail and follow it into the Curious Valley, gouged by a meltwater river from the Pleistocene glacier.

Turn left on the Marshall's Hill Trail and left again on the Indian Trail, which shortly changes name to Red Town Trail. Pause at the Red Town Ballpark, where the Newcastle town team played Black Diamond, Renton,

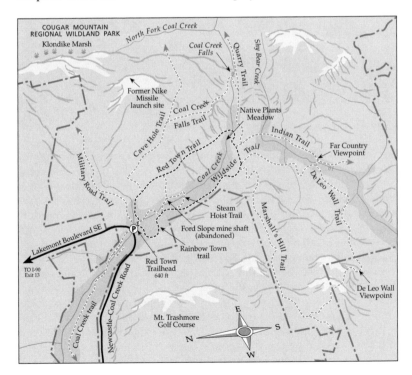

Coal Creek

Franklin, and other competitors in the Coal Country League. Come in April through June for the climax flowering of the ball field in its new role as the Native Plants Meadow, the largest such within 40 miles of Seattle, lovingly tended by volunteers of the Issaquah Alps Trails Club and Washington Native Plants Society and staff of King County Parks. The prairie-meadow displays 88 species of riparian, meadow, and woodland herbs, shrubs, and trees. (Come in fall for the tawny glory of hip-high bunchgrass—tufted hair grass—which you never see in lawns or golf courses.)

Follow the Red Town Trail back through the Curious Valley to Red Town, biggest of the Newcastle neighborhoods. (Others were Rainbow Town, White Town, Finn Town, and Greek Village.) Pass the Cave Hole Trail (—or don't; if you have another hour or three, climb it to Coal Creek Falls, Klondike Marsh, Anti-Aircraft Peak, the Fantastic Erratic). Descend Hill Street past the Superintendent's House and Hospital and Doctor's House and Saloon to the Red Town gate.

2 | SQUAK MOUNTAIN STATE PARK: CENTRAL PEAK TRAIL–EAST SIDE TRAIL

Loop trip: 5 miles
Hiking time: Allow 3½ hours
High point: 2024 feet
Elevation gain: 1300 feet
Hikable: All year
Map: Green Trails No. 2035, Cougar Mountain, Squak Mountain

There is within the hard core of devout Issaquah Alpinists a fanatic sub-group, a cabal of Gnostics, who zealously preach that of all the Issaquah beasts, Squak is the noblest. It has a splendid vastness of primeval forest, and much of the rest was so lightly high-graded that only the scattering of monster stumps reveals that it is not virgin, on the brink of ancient. The short shrift given by the loggers is largely due to the most wicked cliffs in the Alps, carved by the Canadian ice squeezing through canyons. Thanks

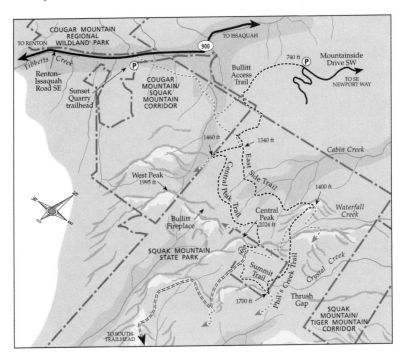

Alders line an abandoned road, now a trail

to these factors (and the preservation ethic of the Bullitt family), it has what may be the fullest representation of native woodland plants in the Alps. As for wilderness, it has some of the wildest. On a densely foggy day in the pre-guidebook, pre-map era of the 1970s I wandered for hours, this way and that and this way again, and rejoiced when I took a tumble on one of those wicked cliffs because then I could at least tell up from down. The trail system is superb—but intricate. Do not come exploring without a big bag of cake crumbs. Or the map.

Early in the new millennium the Issaquah Parks Department, with help of volunteers, will develop two new trailheads, one on the west from the abandoned Sunset Quarry, and the other on the northeast, close to downtown Issaquah and the Metro buses. Until then the most useful trailhead for hikers is reached from the west edge of downtown Issaquah. (The trailhead north of the Sunset Quarry is not advised because of poor and dangerous parking on State Highway 900.)

In Issaquah, from the stoplight at the intersection of W Sunset Way and SE Newport Way, turn steeply uphill on Mountain Park Boulevard SW. Follow it, climbing steadily, twisting and turning, to the leveling out on the crest of the mountain's north ridge. Turn a sharp left onto Mountainside Drive SW and climb a bit more. When the street switchbacks left for still more climbing, go right on a stub to a dead end with very limited parking, elevation 740 feet.

The tour suggested here is a good, straightforward introduction. You'll pass a bushel of junctions. Or maybe you won't pass them? How many cake crumbs are in your bag? Enough for overnight?

Begin with ¾ mile upward on the road (now trail, and wheelfree) that once was the access to the Bullitt summer cabin, now long gone, only the monumental fireplace remaining. At the two junctions you pass, stay left. (The right turns lead down to the State Highway 900 trailhead that we recommend against.) Shortly after the second junction, at 1340 feet, pass the East Side Trail to the left (route of your loop return) and go right, continuing ¼ mile to another junction at 1460 feet. Make a sharp reverse-turn left onto the Central Peak Trail, which in 1 mile culminates in the tower colony atop 2024-foot Central Peak, 2 miles from the car. Slots slashed in the forest to let the microwaves in and out give the trip's only considerable views.

For the 3-mile loop return, from the towers descend the service road ¼ mile and dodge off left and steeply down a path ¼ mile to Phil's Creek Trail, 1700 feet. Turn left, contouring, passing stringers of a long-gone bridge, on the grade of narrow-gauge logging trucks of the 1920s. When the trail dead-ends at brush-obscured relics of an ancient tie mill, a connector path to the right drops straight down to the East Side Trail, 1400 feet; go left for a delightful sidehill saunter homeward through big trees over lovely creeks.

3 TIGER MOUNTAIN STATE FOREST

Maps: Issaquah Alps Trails Club, *Trails of Tiger Mountain*; Green Trails No. 2045 Tiger Mountain

As a freshman at the University of Washington, looking from campus out over Lake Washington, I was startled by how close the mountains came to the city. That they were, indeed, genuine mountains I knew because atop one blinked an airways beacon, westernmost in the line that in the 1930s–1940s guided airmail planes and "Lucky Lindys" trying their luck over the hump at night.

Big Tree trail

The distinction of being the "most-climbed peak in the state," for years accorded Mount Si, began to come into dispute in 1966, when The Mountaineers included East Tiger Mountain in the epochal *100 Hikes in Western Washington*. The abandoned fire lookout tower was still there—but not in 1967, the authorities having hastened to forestall inevitable tragedy by demolishing the rickety ladderway. My first attempt on what the old U.S. Geological Survey map then still in print labeled "Issaquah Mountain" was in the 1950s, via what we climbers, familiar with narratives of attempts on the highest mountain in the world, dubbed the "Great Central Couloir." Deep

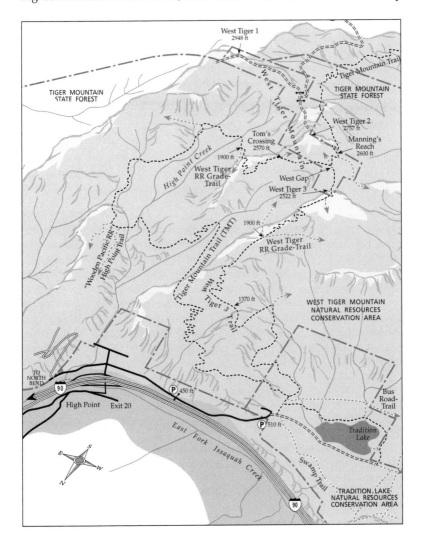

snow defeated me, even as thin air had Smythe on Mt. Everest. Mummery, I think it was, said a peak evolves "from impossible, to experts only, to easy day for a lady." True of the Matterhorn and Grepon, then of Everest, so it was of Issaquah Mountain, known to us now as West Tiger Mountain, site of that guiding blink in the era when I and all of young male America wore Lindy helmets, the light now replaced by a thicket of over-communication towers.

Tiger (East) drew its first crowd in 1966, Tiger (West) in 1969, with Janice Krenmayr's *Footloose Around Puget Sound.* When Janice moved on, I picked up the baton with *Footsore 1* and its dozen Tiger hikes, succeeded in 1995 by my and daughter Penny's *Walks and Hikes in the Foothills and Lowlands Around Puget Sound* and its twenty-odd trips. The full banquet (at least 100 miles of walking) is *Guide to Trails of Tiger Mountain,* published by the Issaquah Alps Trails Club, the first edition in 1981, the eighth in 1998, the author now as always the legendary Chief Ranger of the Alps, Bill Longwell.

TRADITION LAKE NATURAL RESOURCES CONSERVATION AREA: TRADITION LAKE LOOP
Loop trip: ½ mile
Hiking time: Allow 1 hour
High point: 500 feet
Elevation gain: None
Hikable: All year

The Tradition Plateau is the place for toddlers—and for their grandpas with game legs, and their great-grandmothers in wheelchairs. It is lakebed-flat (nearly) because of that Pleistocene glacier, which dammed up a great lake and forced the Snoqualmie River to flow through the Issaquah Alps into the lake, dumping delta sediments that constitute an underground reservoir supplying Issaquah with domestic water. In the 1990s the City of Issaquah combined lands of the watershed it owned on the plateau with those of the state Department of Natural Resources as a Natural Resources Conservation Area (NRCA), an adjunct of the West Tiger Mountain NRCA.

Drive I-90 east of Issaquah, and go off Exit 20 to the High Point interchange. Turn right (west) on the frontage road 0.4 mile to a gate, elevation 450 feet. Park here if you may be returning after dark, when the gate is locked. Otherwise continue 0.6 mile to the large parking area, elevation 510 feet.

The circle around Tradition Lake is everybody's favorite introduction. We say "allow 1 hour," but if you have binoculars, triple that figure: the birding will demand it.

Just as easy-flat and equally well-loved is the 2-mile loop on the Bus Road-Trail, named for the 1940-or-so Greyhound Scenicruiser moldering into the forest floor after completing a second tour of service as chicken house on a long-ago 130-acre homestead. The apple trees are kept thriftily top-pruned by bears.

We speak of "l hour" (or triple that) for the lake loop, but those times are appropriate for the other plateau trails as well, so add the Big Tree Trail, the Brink Trail, the Adventure Trail, the Round Lake Wetlands Trail, and the Swamp Trail and you have two or more full wheelfree days afoot.

WEST TIGER MOUNTAIN NATURAL RESOURCES CONSERVATION AREA: WEST TIGER 3 VIA TRADITION TRAIL

Round trip: 5½ miles
Hiking time: Allow 4 hours
High point: 2522 feet
Elevation gain: 2000 feet
Hikable: All year

West Tiger is the "there" that catches the eyes whizzing by on I-90. West Tiger 3, 2522 feet, is the lowest of the three summits—and the best. It juts out in the sky a mere swan dive from Lake Sammamish. It is blasted by

Mount Rainier from Middle Tiger Mountain before the little trees grew up and blocked the view (Harvey Manning photo)

cold storms in winter and hot sun in summer. The thin soil so scarcely covers bedrock andesite that slow-growing trees are pseudo-alpine; June turns on a mountain-meadow-like glow of lupine, tiger lily, ox-eye daisy, and spring gold. The views are a geography book, an enormous relief map from Rainier to what's left of St. Helens to Olympics, to Si and Baker and Shuksan; from The Narrows to Elliott Bay to Admiralty Inlet to Skagit Bay; from Tacoma to Seattle to Everett.

From the Tradition Plateau trailhead, elevation 510 feet, walk the Bus Road-Trail a scant ¾ mile to a Y, turn left, and go steeply up mixed forest on a long-ago logging road. At 1370 feet, a scant 1½ miles from Bus Road-Trail, the road-trail dead-ends and constructed trail sets out upward in comfortable switchbacks.

At 2-plus miles, 1900 feet, the trail crosses the West Tiger Railroad Grade-Trail; in the 1920s, this was the "lokie logger" route for transporting big sticks to the tramway (the "Wooden Pacific Railroad"), which lowered them to the mill at High Point. The way quickly emerges into views over Grand Ridge and the Snoqualmie Valley to the Cascades and proceeds through coniferous shrubbery, over andesite rubble (or, when winter winds blow from the North Pole, drifted snow), and up the ridge crest, in ½ mile from the railroad grade reaching the summit.

For an epiphany, stay for the sunset over Seattle, Puget Sound, and the Olympics—assuming you have parked outside the gate.

WEST TIGER MOUNTAIN NATURAL RESOURCES CONSERVATION AREA: TIGER MOUNTAIN TRAIL— NORTH END TO MANNING'S REACH
Round trip: 11 miles
Hiking time: Allow 6 hours
High point: 2600 feet
Elevation gain: 2100 feet
Hikable: All year (weather permitting)

October 13, 1979. On this day, culminating seven and a half years in the thinking and three and a half in construction, some 300 person-days of labor and an outlay of public funds of $0.00, the Issaquah Alps Trails Club gathered around chief architect and engineer and trail boss Bill Longwell to celebrate the Grand Opening of the Tiger Mountain Trail (TMT). A group of pundits sponsored by an Eastern foundation arrived soon after to complete a survey of urban-area trails from coast to coast. We took them on an end-to-end walk, at the conclusion of which they pronounced the TMT "the greatest near-city wildland trail in the nation."

The customary way to do the classic end-to-end, 16 miles and 3000 feet of elevation gained, is in a single one-way day, using a two-car shuttle. In ordinary weather it's a good bit of exercise; when the clouds dump deep snow and the polar winds do blow it's survival time. Personally I recommend that before attempting the end-to-end you sample the TMT from the north trailhead to the highest point of the route, 2600 feet. (I first got there, guided by Bill's field notes, in 1977, the first "civilian" to do so, which is why Bill put my name on it. Subsequently I joined his digger corps often enough to earn my union card.)

Start from the Tradition Plateau parking area, elevation 510 feet, walk on the Bus Road-Trail, turn left on the West Tiger 3 Trail, and quickly left again on the TMT. Ascend mixed forest grown rich and mellow since the railroad logging three-quarters of a century ago, pass small waterfalling creeks, then enter alder-maple forest only just beginning the succession to conifers. Around a spur ridge of West Tiger 3 the atmosphere is transformed from deciduous light-and-airy to coniferous shadowed-and-somber—a virgin forest. The route swings into the jungle wet of a deep canyon, bridges a branch of High Point Creek, and climbs out of the canyon to bridge the main branch in a wider, deeper

Round Lake

canyon. Just beyond milepost 13 the way intersects a trail up from High Point, the earliest route taken by the TMT and long before that the line of the "Wooden Pacific Railway," the tram that lifted lokies up to and lowered logs down from the West Tiger Railroad Grade-Trail. This junction, 2½ miles from the trailhead, is a good turnaround for an afternoon's lesson in forest succession.

Cross the West Tiger Railroad Grade-Trail at 1900 feet and continue upward to the high-in-the-sky opens of Tom's Crossing, 2570 feet, on the north ridge of West Tiger 2, then reenter woods to pass through West Gap, 2500 feet, and swing around the side of 2, above the summit of 3, to the highest point of the TMT, 2600 feet, at Manning's Reach, 5½ miles from the north trailhead, 10½ from the south. Take your ease on the bench built for Manning by the kindly Chief Ranger and survey the lower world.

Return to the Tradition Plateau by the TMT or the West Tiger 3 trails— or any of the many other alternatives mapped and described in Bill's book.

4 | TAYLOR MOUNTAIN FOREST

Round trip: Up to 10 miles
Hiking time: Allow up to all day
High point: 2000 feet
Elevation gain: 1220–1450 feet (depending on trailhead)
Hikable: All year
Map: Green Trails No. 2045, Tiger Mountain (*Note:* This
   map shows old logging roads that have been used as
   trails and does *not* depict the ultimate trail system)

The 1700 acres of Taylor Mountain acquired in 1997 by King County are at
an ending and a beginning. Ended are to-the-last-bush clearcutting and
free-for-all fun featuring gunpowder and gasoline. Beginning is an era of
"New Forestry" coexisting with schoolroom-type education and passive
recreation. Highest priority of all is preservation of natural (if necessary,
restored) ecosystems, wildlife habitats, and high-quality water.

The hiker and equestrian can continue to take their pleasure just as they
have for years—but will have more of it because frontier-rowdy play is
banned. The master plan currently in preparation will put to bed some of

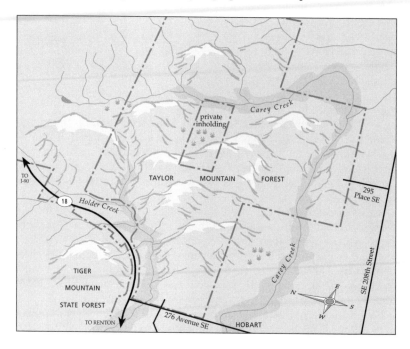

the old logging roads, reduce others to multi-use, and possibly specify some for restricted use, such as "hiker only" or "hiker and horse only."

The entryways are gated; parking areas and trailhead signs will be provided in future. At present an unofficial access point is on the Issaquah-Hobart Road (276 Avenue SE) about ¼ mile south of Highway 18, just beyond Holder Creek at SE 188th Street, elevation 550 feet. Another entry is a scant 2½ miles east of the Issaquah-Hobart Road on SE 208 Street at 295 Place SE, elevation 780 feet.

The future network of official trails will ascend to a highest point of 2000 feet. North of that 1½ miles, outside the county forest, is the 2520-foot western tip of the summit ridge, which runs east 1½ miles to the summit of Taylor Mountain, 2602 feet. Trails in the forest will follow 5 miles on or near banks of Holder and Carey Creeks, headwaters of Issaquah Creek and spawning grounds for species that badly need them. Adjacency to the closed-to-the-public Cedar River Watershed will permit connection (via underpasses to be built) of that "wildlife reservoir" to other peaks of the

Entrance gate to Taylor Mountain road-trails

Issaquah Alps. Trails in the forest may be linked to Tiger and Rattlesnake Mountains, the Cedar River downstream to Renton, and neighboring lands—including (it is hoped) the summit ridge of Taylor and its long view south along the Cascade front to the Osceola Mudflow and Mount Rainier.

Note to hikers who wish to get involved in the development of Taylor Mountain Forest: Though the master plan is not complete, King County Parks is maintaining the site, and meeting regularly with a group of interested neighbors and park users. If you want to contribute your opinions to the master plan, or volunteer to do site restoration or trailwork, contact King County Parks at 206-296-4232 and ask about the "Friends of Taylor Mountain" group.

(It hardly needs to be said that even after the master plan is adopted by the King County Council, an action that will take more than a minute or two, construction of parking lots and trails will depend on future budget decisions. A lot of things have been planned around the county that have not been done, awaiting—often for years—the funding. As for the regional trail connectors on the wish list, they will require interjurisdictional effort—and funding. All the more reason for hikers and trail advocates to get involved.)

5 RATTLESNAKE MOUNTAIN SCENIC AREA: RATTLESNAKE LEDGE

Round trip: 2 miles
Hiking time: Allow 3 hours
High point: 2078 feet
Elevation gain: 1160 feet
Hikable: All year
Map: GreenTrails No. 2055 Rattlesnake Mountain

In the 1950s, on our way to Snoqualmie Pass to perform heroic feats, we used to fix ambitious eyes on the formidable cliff at the east end of Rattlesnake Mountain. Eventually we mounted an expedition, fully equipped with ropeware and ironware and lacking only one of our friend Fred Beckey's crossbows. We never got there. Chunks of the wall that had fallen into the forest waylaid us. They were too towering to be mere boulders. Thus we named them the Rattlesnake Towlders and spent the day performing heroic feats.

Another day, another expedition, and fingers clutched the wall—and came away holding pieces of rubble cemented loosely by moss. So we rounded the corner and scrambled up a brushy gully. And lo! From the north brink of the Ledge, we looked out over the North Bend Plain to the hugeness of Si. From the south brink we looked out over the Cedar River to MacDonald and the Osceola Mudflow. From the east brink we looked up the Middle Fork Snoqualmie to Russian Buttes and Garfield, up the South Fork to and beyond the portal peaks of Mailbox and Washington, and up the Cedar to Chester Morse Reservoir.

We were entertained by the "gravel cirque" in the moraine of the Pleistocene glacier that separates the valley of the Cedar from that of the Snoqualmie. In 1918 Seattle City Water, ignoring geologists who warned that moraine gravel is permeable, filled its new reservoir too full and the "Boxley Burst" blew out the side of the moraine, washing 2,000,000 cubic yards of glacial drift down Boxley Creek, obliterating the town of Edgewick. That's why Seattle built the barbwire fence where they did, in Snoqualmie drainage—not to guard the purity of Cedar water, but to conceal the blunder. That's why, in 1961, a "sanitary patrolman" nabbed me on a return from the Ledge and slapped me with a $25 ticket for climbing over the fence.

Then, in 1976, as I was whining to a Weyerhaeuser forester about the insanity and injustice of it all, he interrupted, "Why, there's a trail now! Seattle moved its fence, the kids at North Bend High did the building, and everybody goes up for picnics!" Triumphantly I returned and wrote up the kids' trail (not exactly a garden path, but legal) for *Footsore 2*, published in 1978.

Go off I-90 on Exit 32 and drive 436 Avenue SE (Cedar Falls Road) 2.7 miles to Rattlesnake Lake, elevation 920 feet. Walk the trail (gated road) to the far side of the lake and the true-trail trailhead, signed "Rattlesnake Lake" and the credits "Issaquah Alps Trails Club and Seattle City Water."

This is not the high school trail, but a new one on the general line of our

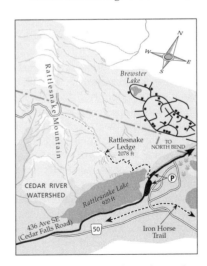

Rattlesnake Ledge

North Bend and Mount Si from Rattlesnake Ledge

old brush-scramble route. It was built by the Rattlesnake Rangers (Issaquah Alps and Snoqualmie Valley Trails Clubs) in preparation for the 1990 Mountains-to-Sound March. Switchbacks climb steeply and steadily through second-growth forest, passing huge mossy-ferny boulders tumbled from the wall, which was over-steepened by the Canadian glacier when it scraped past the eastern tip of the mountain. The top of the Ledge, 2078 feet, a scant mile from the lake, is a broad flat—but the brinks are vertiginous enough to give the dizzies to a mountain goat. Distinctly not a spot for kiddies to toddle or dogs to romp unleashed.

The quieter days are the best for the botanical mind. The winter winds shearing around the corner and the summer sun blasting the near-naked rock create so severe a microclimate that flowers are, despite the low elevation, amazingly subalpine, a color extravaganza when paintbrush and tiger lily and penstemon and phlox and lupine and California tea are in bloom.

6 CEDAR BUTTE

Round trip (from temporary trailhead): 3 miles
Hiking time: Allow 2 hours
High point: 1880 feet
Elevation gain: 900 feet
Hikable: All year
Map: Green Trails No. 2065 Mt. Washington

The U.S. Coast and Geodetic Survey summit benchmark says "1937 CEDER BUTT." The loggers who did the scalping called it "Old Baldy." In the era when *The Mountaineer* was reporting the Wagnerian first ascents of Forbidden, Formidable, Terror, and Despair, its pages also noted a "Herpicide Spire," employing the generic term (misspelled) for weedkiller, which the droll "firsters" felt should be applied to finish the job started by logging and fire; the misuse of "spire" was, of course, deliberately blasphemous. The Firster Greats of the time devoted considerable detective work to ferreting out the location and identity of the "spire." Outraged by the lese majesty, they suppressed the nascent fame of Herpicide.

In the 1950s the secret was revealed to a group of climbers whose feats I subsequently recounted in an article for *The Mountaineer*, "Things to Climb When Mountains Aren't Worth It." Among our exploits were conquest of

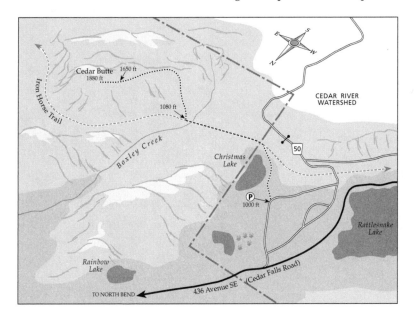

the "things" that later (in 1976) were transformed for political purposes (by me) from Issaquah Blobs to Issaquah Alps. The North Bend Blobs, though, remained just that. Tom Miller bought U.S. Army blanket pins, one cent apiece, at the Co-op (as REI was then known, because its original name was Recreational Equipment Cooperative), burned on the words "Blob Peak Pin," and awarded them to those who "summited" (a repulsive neologism that had not yet been misbegotten).

Fuller Mountain, Little Si—and Herpicide Spire. Hundreds, perhaps thousands of Mountaineers have been awarded the treasured Six Peak Pin; no more than a half dozen have qualified for the Blob Peak Pin, partly because most Mountaineers don't recognize a butt even when on top of one, but mostly because the location of the Spire remained a closely held secret. Pete

Mailbox Peak from Cedar Butte

Schoening, one of the half dozen, is internationally renowned for deeds in the Karakoram and Antarctica, but for those he got no pins.

Go off I-90 on Exit 32 and drive 436 Avenue SE (Cedar Falls Road) toward Rattlesnake Lake, which will be the Iron Horse trailhead when Seattle City Water implements plans now in development. Until then, at ¼ mile short of the entry house at the lake, turn off left on a wide gravel road. Park at the first sharp bend. To the right spot the barbwire fence on concrete posts marking the watershed boundary, elevation 1000 feet.

The trail follows the fence, skirting Christmas Lake to the Puget Sound Energy powerline access road. Follow the road up to the old Milwaukee mainline, now the Iron Horse Trail, which is reached about 1 mile east of the to-be permanent trailhead.

Turn left on the grade ¼ mile to Boxley Creek. Beyond the bridge pass two power poles; short of the third, look right and spy the start of the trail, elevation 1080 feet.

Cross, then recross, an old logging grade. From the recrossing, the main trail straightforwardly sets out straight up. The more interesting alternative turns right on the grade to the Boxley Burst (Hike 5, Rattlesnake Ledge). Follow the blowout around left to near the ridge top. In a swale, 1650 feet, rejoin the main trail to climb steeply to the summit, 1880 feet.

The Spire lifts conspicuously from the moraine of the Canadian glacier. At the moraine's east end rises Mt. Washington, the Cascade front. On the west end is Rattlesnake Ledge, terminus of the Issaquah Alps. North across the North Bend Plain (lakebed dating from that Pleistocene business) stands Si. South is the Cedar River valley, featuring the Masonry Pool, Chester Morse Reservoir (the drowned Cedar Lake), and Little Mountain, which is reputed never to have been climbed except by loggers.

Big Si from Little Si

MIDDLE FORK SNOQUALMIE RIVER

Newcomers to the Middle Fork have exclaimed, "If this valley was near any other American city, it would long ago have been a national park!" If I may be excused for quoting myself, I expressed the thought in 1978, in *Footsore 2*:

> *The center ring, the big business, the heart of the matter, the real Snoqualmie, is the Middle Fork. One need only scan a map and note from what great peaks it flows, what a vast basin it drains, how long is its valley and—in the lower reaches of the U-shaped glacial trough—how wide, to realize this is the main show. . . . In obedience to the maxim that Closer is Better, the recreational potential of the Cascade front should be exploited more enthusiastically. Where the rivers emerge from the mountains there should be Cascade Gateway Recreation Areas abounding in picnic grounds and campgrounds and trails served by buses from the major clumps of population. Lots of hikers lots of times would prefer closer-to-home exercise than that available in high mountains of the Cascade Crest. And they would appreciate trails that are snowfree all or most of the year, rather than just late summer and early fall. And they would not invariably insist on thrashing fragile alpine-wilderness ecosystems; often they'd be happy in tougher, more boot-resistant terrain. This is not mere theory—observe the mobs milling around the North Bend vicinity looking for something to do. It's rather pitiful to see the manswarms (and womanswarms and childrenswarms) marching in lockstep up the Mount Si trail. They should have three dozen alternatives in the same neighborhood.*

Well, now they do, or nearly, and I like to think *Footsore* contributed. But just as guns don't kill people, books don't activate political machinery; people do. It has happened—is happening.

Mount Baker–Snoqualmie National Forest, once known only as a custodian of remote woods, the last of the American frontier, has begun to adjust to the changed responsibilities of life on the city edge. The state Department of Natural Resources, formerly content to take its marching orders from the forest industry, is becoming a people-sensitive and socially innovative public lands manager.

The government agencies noted above, and others representing cities and counties, and others charged with wildlife protection and ecosystem preservation, are engaged in a Middle Fork Snoqualmie River Study, the aim being to develop a River Corridor Public Use Concept, to be implemented by a Middle Fork River Council, an interagency coordinating committee.

A number of citizen groups concerned by the management chaos have formed the Middle Fork Outdoor Recreation Coalition (MidFORC), combining the massed forces of the Alpine Lakes Protection Society, the North Cascades Conservation Council, the Sierra Club, The Mountaineers, Washington Trails Association, Seattle Audubon Society, Washington Native Plants Society, and others.

If recreation of the flesh and re-creation of spirit are high on the agenda of

Otter Falls and Lipsy Lake

Study and Concept and Council, so too is the traditional role of exploiting natural resources. Here the Department of Natural Resources (DNR) is leading the way. In 1993 the state Legislature passed legislation embodying a new concept, that of the Natural Resources Conservation Area, patterned on the National Wilderness Act of 1964. The twenty-one land units initially given the special status include Mount Si NRCA, companion of the West Tiger Mountain NRCA. Resource extraction is virtually excluded in favor of wildlife habitat, gene-pool reserves, water quality, landscape preservation, education, research, and low-impact (note the emphasis) recreation; natural ecosystems take precedence over every anthropocentric exploitation, not excluding fun and games.

By transfers among DNR-managed trust lands and by exchange for and purchase of private lands, a good start has been made toward placing a projected 10,000 acres, nearly 16 square miles, in the Mount Si NRCA. Part will be "new wilderness" ("reclaimed" or "re-created"), where past logging on high-elevation "tree farms" (actually, cellulose mines) has flushed so much soil down the streams that another "crop" could not grow in less than a millennium. Part will be pristine wilderness, where cliffs have protected ancient forests from saws. In both old and new, the crush of commerce and heavy recreation will yield to the light-and-quiet recreations that accept the primacy of wild plants and creatures, of waters and rocks.

However, complementary to outright set-aside is the DNR development of a "new forestry" policy designed to save the forest industry from self-destruction. Again, the pattern has been set by Tiger Mountain State Forest, where subeconomic forests have been placed in the wilderness-like NRCA; the rest, where trees can thrive, are managed for *genuine* sustained yield and *genuine* multiple use.

Preparing for its new responsibilities in urban-edge wildland-backcountry, the Mount Baker–Snoqualmie National Forest released in 1999 an Environmental Assessment and Travel Management Plan for the 110,000-acre valley. The implementations sought by a broad consensus of wilderness organizations include:

1. Add to the Alpine Lakes Wilderness the entire Pratt River valley and its peaks; the valley walls and summits of the Middle Fork southeast of the lower river (Mailbox Peak to Taylor River); and valley walls and summits south of the upper river (Taylor River upstream to existing Alpine Lakes Wilderness).
2. Exclude vehicles from the upper valley.
3. Provide multi-use trails in the area northwest of the Middle Fork as fa' upstream as Taylor River; limit travel in the areas destined ultimately for the Alpine Lakes Wilderness (noted above) to hiker-horse travel. Most multi-use will be confined to the extensive system of abandon(logging roads. (Construction of any new multi-use trails, as well as hiker-horse trails, will be subject to constraints imposed by needs t preserve wildlife habitat and stream-water quality.)

7 | LITTLE SI

Round trip from bridge: 5 miles
Hiking time: Allow 3 hours
High point: 1576 feet
Elevation gain: 1200 feet
Hikable: All year
Maps: Green Trails No. 174 Mount Si, No. 206 Bandera

Mount Si's footstool peaklet is as old as the Canadian glacier that rode over and around it, smoothing and plucking, as old as the seismic shakings that thrust up the Moon Wall and this lesser by-blow, and for a century (or millennia?) people have been scrambling to the summit to gaze out upon the North Bend Plain.

However, until 1985 there never was a trail, only boot-scrubbed rocks of the scrambling route. With DNR authorization I asked Will Thompson, a Hard-Core Ptarmigan famed for 1930s explorations in the North Cascades, to take a look. Will looked—and flagged, and built, ¾ mile of new trail. Mind you, this was a volunteer labor, no machinery or dynamite, just plain muscle. Parents who do not like to push and pull kids over logs and rocks may find the way up the Big easier than the Little.

Drive I-90 to Exit 31 and go off into North Bend. From the center of town, go right on SE North Bend Way 0.8 mile, then left on Mt. Si Road 0.3 mile, across the Middle Fork Bridge.

Now, *pay close attention:* As this edition goes to press, the procedure is to take an immediate left on 434 Avenue SE to a smallish fishermens' parking

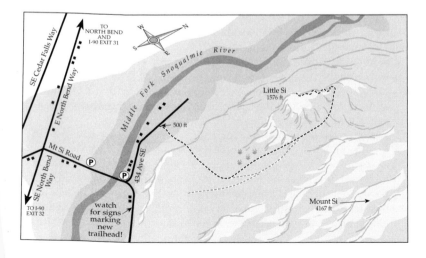

View south of Little Si

lot, elevation 500 feet. The parking lot will probably be full, but don't seek space on 434th, it's full-up with homes. Instead, retreat across the bridge and find a spot along the shoulder.

Watch for possible prominent signs directing you to a new trailhead being planned farther south along the Mt. Si Road. This, of course, will entail a different route for the approach to Little Si from that described in the next paragraph. Until then, walk ¼ mile from the bridge on 434th to a signed trail, on the right.

A start on the valley floor gives way to a huff-puff up the valley wall. At ⅓ mile is a split; go left. Or, if you like, stay right to the next split in ⅛ mile more and go left there. *Somewhere in the vicinity the new trail will be encountered, sooner or later.*

The splits unite to go from mixed forest grown up since logging in the 1960s to virgin forest grown up since the fires that swept most of Little and Big Si in the nineteenth century. No, the trees are not big and ancient—this is the look of a *young* virgin forest. A swamp bowl extends to the base of the cliffs. Spur trails branch left. Ignore them—they don't go the way you want to.

From the 1930s to the 1950s, the Climbing Course of The Mountaineers utilized Little Si for basic rock practice—or, as sardonic students called it, "moss and mud practice." Drier, cleaner, sounder rock was found and these *mountain* climbers joyously fled the scene. But in the 1990s the vacancy was filled by "sport climbers" who flocked to indoor "sport walls" and, outdoor, to every bit of steep, exposed rock visible from and handy to a major highway. That's what those ropes and hardware and gaudy costumes are doing up there, hanging in the air above the trail.

Stay right, ascending into the rift where the glacier squeezed through. The ice seems scarcely to have melted, so chilly it is here, where the sun so rarely shines. Giant boulders tumbled from above are strewn through the dark forest, and beneath the boulders are trogs. One becomes aware of the cliff close left—and then of a cliff overhead! It is the Great Overhang, often admired from I-90 but shocking to be discovered hanging heavy, heavy over thy head! The trail ascends over a low, forested rib, then descends briefly before the final assault on the summit and splendid views out to North Bend Plain and Mt. Washington, Mailbox Peak, and Rattlesnake Mountain.

8 | MOUNT SI

Round trip to cliff viewpoint: 2 miles
Hiking time: Allow 2 hours
High point: 1600 feet
Elevation gain: 850 feet
Hikable: All year

Round trip to Snag Flat: 3½ miles
Hiking time: Allow 4 hours
High point: 2100 feet
Elevation gain: 1350 feet
Hikable: All year

Round trip to Haystack Basin: 8 miles
Hiking time: Allow 8 hours
High point: 3900 feet
Elevation gain: 3200 feet
Hikable: March–November
Maps: Green Trails No. 174 Mount Si, No. 206 Bandera

Had Nature installed Mount Si anywhere east of the Rocky Mountains, chances are it would have been America's first national park. Immigrants fresh off the boat from Europe hardly could have failed to accord the upthrust the same respect as the Original Inhabitants, domiciled in Western

North Bend from Mount Si

Washington ten or a dozen millennia. Any new arrival could plainly see that the mountain and the nearby falls were designated spots to listen attentively to the spirits of the sky. The mountain surely was in a position to speak for these spirits, inasmuch as it actually was the Moon, fallen from the sky to earth. (The object that has taken its former place is an impostor.)

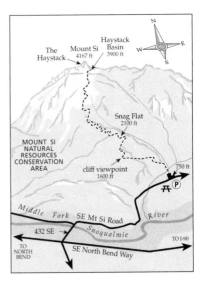

Almost since this majestic hunk was named for an 1862 settler, Josiah Merritt ("Uncle Si"), it has drawn hikers. After being for generations the best-known (well, perhaps second to Rainier) and most-climbed (by some 50,000 a year) mountain in the state, it received overdue recognition as the superstar of a Natural Resources Conservation Area, flagship for a wildly exciting new concept in management of state lands.

Drive SE Mt. Si Road (Hike 7,

Little Si) 2 miles from the Middle Fork Snoqualrnie River bridge to the enormous trailhead parking lot, elevation 750 feet.

From low-valley lushness of hardwood-conifer forest, the trail ascends the steep valley wall to a nineteenth-century burn featuring a new forest of firs up to 2 feet thick, plus huge black snags of the old forest. In 1 long mile, at 1600 feet, a rock slab-cliff (a glacier job) opens a window to the valley floor, to I-90, to the moraine of the Canadian glacier sweeping in an arc from the Middle Fork valley over the South Fork to the Cedar River.

In ¾ mile more, at 2100 feet, the way levels at Snag Flat's grove of Douglas firs; though fire-blackened, they were big enough to survive the conflagrations that denuded most of Si in the nineteenth century and remote enough to escape the loggers. However, weakened by fire they at last are succumbing and most are snagtops. Here in the ancient-forest gloom, beside the lovely creek, is a pleasant spot for picnicking, a satisfying winter–early spring turnaround.

Usually in March or April (often earlier), the snow melts on the higher slopes. The trail can then be climbed 2⅓ more miles to Haystack Basin, 3900 feet, 4 miles. Clamber around the boulders under the wall of The Haystack, 4167-foot final peak of Si. But don't climb it unless you know what you're doing—and even if you do, don't climb it when other people are around; there is danger of being hit by falling bodies.

From the edge of the fault scarp plunging more than 3000 feet to the valley, admire the green pastures, the geometry of streets in North Bend and Snoqualmie, the sprawling new suburbs, the world-class golf courses, the bugs scurrying along I-90, and the panorama from Rainier to Rattlesnake Mountain to the Issaquah Alps, and on to towers of downtown Seattle and the Olympics.

9 | MOUNT TENERIFFE

Round trip: 14 miles
Hiking time: Allow 10 hours
High point: 4788 feet
Elevation gain: 4000 feet
Hikable: May–November
Map: Green Trails No. 174 Mount Si

The largest of the Canary Islands is Teneriffe (also spelled with a single f). A 12,192-foot volcanic peak on the island is named Mt. Teyde, or Teide, and also called the Peak of Tenerife. I have no idea how the companion of Si got a Canary connection. This titillation aside, the attraction lies in the fact that on a day when the Si trail is bumper to bumper from trailhead to

Haystack, Teneriffe may be lonesome. As with Si, a person needn't go to the top for a wealth of views.

Drive SE Mt. Si Road (Hike 7, Little Si) 2 miles from the Middle Fork Snoqualmie River bridge to the Big Si trailhead and then 1.1 miles more to "School Bus Turnaround." Reverse-turning to the left is a woods road. The gate has been eternally shut to public vehicles since the late 1980s. Park here, elevation 950 feet. (In the near future a large trailhead parking area will be provided hereabouts, serving both Teneriffe and the CCC Road-Trail.)

The Teneriffe road-trail sidehills forest and stumps west 2 miles, ascending gradually to 1300 feet. The old map shows the "jeep trail" (leading to somebody's "mine") crossing a nameless intermittent stream. In the mid-1960s a textbook case of illegal (then merely immoral) logging practices destabilized the headwaters. The first in a continuing series of hell-roaring blowouts gouged a boggling canyon and swept down to the Snoqualmie thousands of tons of soil that nevermore will grow forest. The replacement road built to scalp the ridge refrained from crossing Hell-Roaring Nameless Canyon—until just above the spot where loggers triggered the blowout.

At 3200 feet, 2 steep, switchbacking miles from the 1300-foot level, the consciousness expands as the road-trail emerges from virgin forest into the 1960s Georgia-Pacific clearcut, which even now catches the eyes (and perhaps opens them wide) of the I-90 traveler. The clearcut opens a panorama from Rattlesnake Mountain to McClellan Butte, Rainier rising above it all. The I-90 route up the moraine holds a fascination; the morbid ear dwells on the loudness of the roar even this high.

Far enough? If not, continue switchbacking up in new-growing forest,

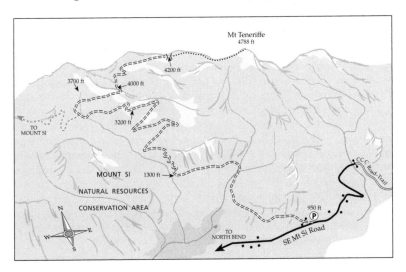

Green Mountain from Mount Teneriffe

which in the NRCA never again will hear the whine of the chainsaw. Avoid a spur left to Si, whose Haystack soon appears, the top almost invariably occupied by a bunch of human bananas. At about 3700 feet the proper route heads east. The trick here is to not climb too high too soon. Do not take spurs toward the ridge crest; choose the road-trail that swings around the jut of a prominent spur ridge at 4000 feet to a big-view promontory and, in spring, a big snowbank. Dropping to round the head of a shallow little valley, the way then climbs to a 4200-foot saddle, 2 miles from the 3200-foot view-point. Views, now, down to Rachor Lake and the North Fork Snoqualmie.

At last the route leaves road and clearcut to follow the rounded crest of the forested summit ridge east on a very faint trail, easy and safe. My favorite season for the ascent is late spring, the trail under snow. After ups and downs and a final short, steep up, in 1 mile the trees shrink and vanish. Mossy rocks of the bald summit are brightened by phlox, lupine, and paintbrush. The 4788-foot summit (which in contrast to Si's treacherous Haystack requires no dangerous scrambling) has a view guaranteed to shut your mouth. The plunge to the valley is longer than from Si. And there is Si to look at, ever growing a fresh crop of bananas. And Washington and McClellan Butte and Mailbox. And Rattlesnake and other Issaquah Alps. And Green, Garfield, Russian Buttes. And peaks of the Cascade Crest, Glacier, Baker, Rainier, and the North Cascades.

10 | CCC ROAD-TRAIL

At the turn of the century a trail for foot and stock ascended the Middle Fork valley to the "gopher holes" of Dutch Miller and his companion swarm of incurable optimists. In the 1920s the locomotive ("lokie") loggers pushed rails past Taylor River to Goldmeyer Hot Springs and up the Pratt River. In the Great Depression, the industry having picked up its tracks and pulled out of the valley, the Civilian Conservation Corps (CCC) arrived to fulfill the Manifest Destiny of America to bring every province of God's earth under man's gas-powered wheels. Starting from what is now Mt. Si Road, the Three Cs bulldozed a truck track up moraines of the Canadian glacier and contoured the valley wall high above the site of the Pleistocene lake, thus avoiding the swamps the railroad had to trestle through, at last descending to join the rail grade near old Camp Brown, just short of the Taylor River.

In the 1960s the loggers returned to cut the virgin forests on valley walls beyond reach of the defunct railroad. CCC Road was pretty much abandoned, replaced on the valley floor by a Middle Fork Road that made CCC Road that much more lonesome. Then the Second-Wave clearcutters of the second growth got to work reskinning the moraines and cleaning up "long

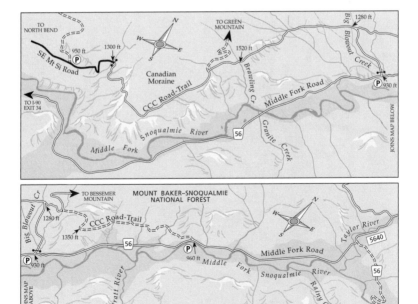

corners" of virgin forest, using every existing road and then some. By the late 1980s the industry had gone about as far as it could go. Again CCC Road fell (pretty) silent. Now and then another patch of trees had to be trucked out, but between such operations the only racketing was by such fun-runners in motorcycles and sports-utility vehicles as Nature deigned to grant passage. In the late 1990s the installation of gate(s) further deepened the peace, and CCC Road-Trail it now is.

WEST ENTRY

Round trip to Big Blowout Creek: 12½ miles
Hiking time: Allow 6 hours
High point: 1620 feet
Elevation gain: 670 feet, loss 240 feet
Hikable: All year
Map: Green Trails No. 174 Mount Si

Drive SE Mt. Si Road (Hike 7, Little Si) south 3.1 miles to the "School Bus Turnaround" at the Teneriffe trailhead, elevation 950 feet. The road continues but is signed "Road Closed—Do Not Enter." Good advice. It steeply climbs 0.9 mile to the far frontier of exurbia at 1300 feet. No parking is possible here, and the CCC Road is gated. So resign yourself to walking that extra mile.

Wintertime view of Russian Butte from CCC Road

Beyond the gate, atop the moraine, the views are enormous, and will continue to be so until a new crop of trees leaps up. Look out over the North Bend Plain to Rattlesnake Mountain; over Grouse Ridge (part of the moraine) to the South Fork valley, framed by the portal peaks of Mailbox and Washington; across and up the broad trough of the Middle Fork (in which flowed, at different times, both the ice from the Cascade Crest and the foreign ice invading from Canada) to the clearcuts of Granite Creek, Teneriffe, Green, and Bessemer, and to the rough-and-rugged Russian Buttes and the Yosemite-like granite walls of Garfield. Until a new forest walls off the scenery, this is a trip in itself. Break out the picnic lunch and eat and look your fill and go home content.

At 2½ miles from the 1300-foot gate is the turnoff to Green Mountain. In ½ mile more is Brawling Creek, 1520 feet, the first in a series of watercourses that regularly flush winter cloudbursts and spring snowmelt from logging-denuded slopes and rip out the road. This is the second scenery banquet, 4 miles from the "School Bus Turnaround" and 600 feet of elevation gain, a pleasant afternoon and a good spot to finish off leftover lunch.

At ⅓ mile from Brawling Creek is a skinny ledge blasted across granite slabs polished smooth by the ice. The views not only are terrific but they never will be blocked by trees because the ledge is at the edge of empty air. Sort of scary when choked by a jackstraw of logs avalanched from the clearcuts above.

In the next 2 miles are continuous broad views, more demented torrents, and finally Big Blowout Creek, 1280 feet. Before Bessemer Mountain was deforested, this was a lively but civil music-maker. Destabilized by the loggers, the stream went stark staring mad—it flows sometimes in a canyon a dozen feet deep, sometimes through a tumble of boulders, and sometimes down a connector road toward the valley road.

MIDDLE ENTRY

Round trip to Brawling Creek: 7 miles
Hiking time: Allow 4 hours
High point: 1520 feet
Elevation gain (on return): 640 feet

Round trip to Tall Moss Cliff: 4½ miles
Hiking time: Allow 5 hours
High point: 1520 feet
Elevation gain: 700 feet, loss 170 feet
Hikable: All year
Map: Green Trails No. 174 Mount Si

This is the best entry for a variety of choices, very short to quite long. The section west from Big Blowout, 1280 feet, to Brawling Creek is the most scenically exciting of the entire route, and is short enough to allow plenty

Pratt River valley from CCC Road

of time for the picnic lunch. The section east leads in ⅓ mile from Big Blowout to the Bessemer Mountain road-trail, and in 1 mile more to Tall Moss Cliff and, below it, a promontory, 1350 feet. In winter, the alder screen deleafed, the views from the promontory are 500 vertical feet down to the river, out the valley to the lowlands, up the valley to Garfield's cliffs, and across to Mount Roosevelt and the Pratt River valley, guarded by the beetling crags of Russian Buttes.

Friends tell us that a bushwacker can find a grove of huge cedars about 1500 feet below Big Blowout Creek. We haven't been there yet.

From I-90 drive Middle Fork Road (Hike 13, Mailbox Peak) 7.4 miles (1.9 miles from the Middle Fork bridge) to a gated sideroad, elevation 930 feet.

Walk the sideroad, which climbs the moraine a long 1 mile to intersect CCC Road at Big Blowout Creek.

EAST ENTRY

Round trip to Tall Moss Cliff: 4 miles
Hiking time: Allow 1 hour
High point: 1450 feet
Elevation gain: 400 feet
Hikable: All year
Map: Green Trails No. 207 Snoqualmie

Drive Middle Fork Road 9.7 miles from I-90 (2.3 miles beyond the Middle-Entry sideroad). Below a cliff, spot a greenery-obscured sideroad. Until the mid-1980s it was signed "CCC Road 1"—odd, because this *is* CCC Road, elevation 960 feet.

The sign is gone. Most motorized wheels are gone, excluded by the huge boulders in the roadbed. The road-that-was narrows to a delightful foot-path-that-is through groves of alder and half-century-old second growth, the forest floor a carpet of moss. At ½ mile the road splits; go left. In a few feet is a stream that may be dangerous to cross in high water. In 1 mile wintertime views begin across the Middle Fork to the Pratt. In a scant 2 miles the way passes Tall Moss Cliff to the 1350-foot saddle, ½ mile and many fine wheelstoppers from Bessemer road-trail.

11 | GREEN MOUNTAIN

Round trip to Absolute Last Promontory: 12 miles
Hiking time: Allow 8 hours
High point: 2900 feet
Elevation gain: 1950 feet
Hikable: February–December
Map: Green Trails No. 174 Mount Si

The next mountain east from Teneriffe is Green. The 4824-foot summit presently lacks a trail and thus is pretty much left alone. However, the road-trail to Absolute Last Promontory is the Middle Fork's best mid-elevation broad-view walk.

Drive I-90 to North Bend (Hike 9, Mt. Teneriffe, and Hike 10, CCC Road-Trail) to the Teneriffe trailhead, elevation 950 feet.

Walk the CCC Road-Trail 3½ miles, to 1514 feet. Turn off left uphill on a grassy sideroad with a rusty old gate half-hidden in the brush. The road climbs a scant ¹⁄₁₀ mile to a Y. Go right, over an intermittent creek to another

Absolute Last Promontory on Green Mountain

Y. Take the right fork steeply uphill. At the second switchback, 2300 feet, leave the road and push through the brush to a big ravine with a wide-angle view down to the U-shaped glacier trough of the Middle Fork, the rolling moraine ridges out in the trough, and buttresses of Russian Buttes. The creek sheets over granite slabs, suggesting foot-washing and other water sports.

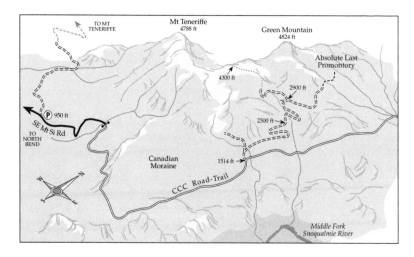

In four more switchbacks, at 2 miles, 2900 feet, the road-trail nears the top of the old clearcut and commences contouring. Soon a very brushy intersection with a profusion of trail-marking tape and a narrow opening through the brush indicate that everyone should go left. Not true, unless you are aiming for the summit (see below). Stay right and thread through alders and all to an esthetic granite outcrop, Far Enough Promontory. Sit on a granite bench thoughtfully provided by Nature and gaze out the valley to Rattlesnake and Rainier, across to Mailbox and Russian Buttes and the mind-boggling clearcuts in Granite Creek, and up the valley to the Pratt River and the granite walls of Garfield. Perhaps continue the contour another ¼ mile to Absolute Last Promontory, 2800 feet, and a close look at close-shaved Bessemer. Perhaps puzzle out the linkage of logging roads and keep going to Bessemer and loop on back via CCC Road-Trail.

If it's the summit you want, at the profusion of tape take the left fork to the end of recognizable trail. Trust the tape. The slope is super-steep and a jungle of huckleberries, devils club, and salmonberry doesn't make things better. For most folks the rubble slopes near 4300 feet suggest it's time for lunch. The views are extraordinary. Continuing onward over loose boulders, angling left to the ridge top and more views; tough work. As for the summit, keep in mind the slogan of Hitler Youth: "To rest is not to conquer." (Whatever happened to those guys?) Maybe you'd be happier waiting for the trail to be built. Of course, if it's solitude you seek, now is the time to go.

12 | SOUTH BESSEMER MOUNTAIN

Round trip: 14 miles
Hiking time: Allow 9 hours
High point: 5000 feet
Elevation gain: 4200 feet
Hikable: April–October
Map: Green Trails No. 174 Mount Si

Thanks to its eminence as the apex of the ridge that starts with Si and continues through Teneriffe and Green, and thanks to savage logging, South Bessemer is the supreme grandstand of the Middle Fork. The devastation is hideous—the Forest Service cringes and reminds the visitor, "Don't blame us, blame the Northern Pacific Land Grant, blame private industry." At lower elevations the second growth since 1950s clearcutting is doing well enough. On high, the 1970s clearcutting is a catastrophe on the geologic scale. Trees 450 years old and only as big as lowland trees grow in thirty years were cut—and fewer than a third were hauled away, the rest

Late-May photo of Bessemer Mountain

left to rot. Streams destabilized by the logging have gone crazy, flushing the mountain's soil to the valley in blowout floods.

Drive I-90 to Exit 34, signed "468 Avenue," go north on 468 Avenue SE 0.4 mile, and turn right on Middle Fork Road. At 7.4 miles from I-90 park near a gated sideroad, elevation 930 feet.

Walk a long 1 mile up to CCC Road-Trail. Turn right ⅓ mile to a Y, 1280 feet. Ascend left on the (gated) Bessemer road-trail. At 2500 feet, 2 miles from CCC Road-Trail, the way abruptly emerges from 1950s second growth into 1970s stumpland and the views become flabbergasting.

To summarize the views: Early on the feature is the broad trough of the Middle Fork and the intricate dissection of the bed of the Pleistocene lake dammed by the glacier from Canada. Next the broad trough of the Pratt River dominates, the catkin-brown (in spring) lines of alder in green second-growth forest plainly showing the logging-railroad grades of the 1920s and 1930s. Then the "Low Sierra" walls of Garfield capture the eye, and the row of icy peaks on the Cascade Crest from Daniel to Chimney Rock to Lemah and smaller peaks of the Snoqualmie Pass area. Finally there is the around-the-compass panorama from the summit—Rainier and Baker, the Olympics and Puget Sound and towers of downtown Seattle, Cougar Mountain, and the Snoqualmie River valley. No trees get in eyes' way.

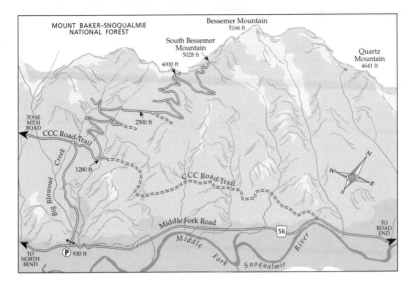

Though the network of logging roads on Bessemer looks formidably intricate from a distance, there's no confusion. Always choose the option that proceeds meaningfully upward, and you can't miss. At about 2 miles from the 2500-foot level, the main road comes within a few feet of a 4000-foot saddle. Keep to the main road 1 final mile to the scalped, bulldozed-flat top of South Bessemer Mountain at 5000 feet. A stone's throw away is the 5028-foot tippy-top, whose patch of scrawny trees presumably was left to seed the crop of the year 3000. North Bessemer, 5166 feet, is a rough mile away. No stroll, that. But check out the possible connections in the other direction, to Green.

13 | MAILBOX PEAK

Round trip: 6 miles
Hiking time: Allow 8 hours
High point: 4841 feet
Elevation gain: 4000 feet
Hikable: April–November
Map: Green Trails No. 206 Bandera

Many a day of early spring, as we drove to Snoqualmie Pass to "push the climbing season" by "postholing" up a peak of the Cascade Crest, sinking in to the knees, changing the lead every dozen postholes, I'd look up to summits at the gateway from the North Bend Plain to the upper South Fork Snoqualmie valley, entranced by a nameless portal mountain whose wide-open-to-the-sun ridge was not only bare of trees (fire, avalanches, whatever) but even in March nearly bare of snow. No postholing there. And the views! At this absolute front of the range, they had to be the equal of those from Si.

But how could you get there? Lo, in *Signpost Magazine* in 1991, Sally Pfeiffer described a trail to the summit, for which she coined the name "Mailbox" because the register book was inside a very old, heavy, green mailbox. Who carried it up there? When? Notes in the box dated to the 1950s; Sally estimated the trail was built no later than 1940.

Warren Jones, long-time prominent member of the North Bend trail intelligentsia, informs me the trail originally started at Vallley (sic) Camp, implying the Lutheran Layman League members probably were the builders. Clearcuts have obliterated this beginning stretch. The first mile of surviving trail may not survive. I here repeat my clarion call for a new trailhead from the State Fire Training Center, at 1600 feet. Some ½ mile of new construction would intersect the existing summit trail (which, by the way, could stand some volunteer attention). Until my call is heeded, the present old start is still it.

Drive I-90 to Exit 34, signed "468th Avenue," and go off north on 468 Avenue SE. At 0.4 mile past the Seattle East Auto Truck Plaza, turn right on Middle Fork Road. When it splits, take either fork; they rejoin in 2.1 miles. Proceed 0.2 mile to pavement's end 2.9 miles from I-90. On the right are a parking area and a gated road, elevation 820 feet.

At a Y in 0.2 mile keep straight ahead. In 0.3 mile more, watch carefully for a wooden sign to the left behind a tree, "4841." More prominent, probably is, a newer sign, "Mailbox Peak." If you pass a small creek you have gone 100 feet too far.

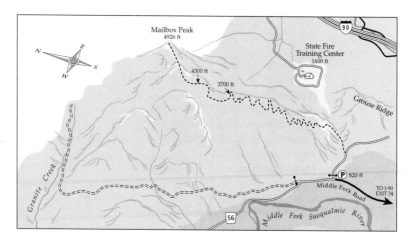

Mailbox Peak. The mailbox has been replaced with a new one.

Don't expect a boulevard. A few volunteers have done some good deeds. Boots that have come march, march, marching since Sally spread the news in 1991 have done more. But don't set out with too light a heart. Ira opines: "This trail is not for everyone. It is rough and varies from steep to very steep to awful steep, and a 4000-foot elevation gain is horrendous for a single day. Further, chances on the descent are excellent for twisting, spraining, or breaking an ankle or knee or leg, if not your head or back."

Only about 300 feet are gained in the first mile through forests of Grouse Ridge. Stepping over a log near a creek signals the impending start of the steep—gaining 3800 feet in 2½ miles, an average of almost 1600 feet a mile. New-built switchbacks end in 1 mile. In the next 1¼ miles, to 3700 feet, the way emerges from forest into semi-naked slopes of the ancient burn, marked by ribbons through shrub-trees, beargrass, and huckleberries to the ridge crest at 4300 feet. A small felsenmeer-rockslide, a field of heather, and then at 4926 feet, behold—the mailbox!

How about those views?

14 | GRANITE LAKES

Round trip to upper lake: 11 miles
Hiking time: Allow 6 hours
High point: 3100 feet
Elevation gain: 2300 feet
Hikable: All year
Map: Green Trails No. 206 Bandera

When first I came to the Granite Lakes, in 1977, I was reminded of photographs of the Western Front, hellish landscapes where armies had bombed and blasted and killed year after year in the Great War. It was as if I had arrived at such a battlefield the day after the guns had gone silent: "the horror, the horror. . . ." This war could not be allowed to continue. The Cascades were going to run out of trees. The public would awake to the crimes. The monsters who were grinding up the American earth like so much hamburger were going to be brought up on charges.

And in 1999? The access road now is firmly gated. Seedlings are springing up wherever any soil remains. "Roses are blooming in Picardy."

Drive from I-90 to the Mailbox Peak trailhead (Hike 13) and park, elevation 820 feet. (Changes are coming; for now, walk the road another 0.2 mile to a gated sideroad that has no room for parking.)

Ascend the road past the gate into pleasant mixed forest grown up since logging of the medium-remote past, views occasionally to valley and moraine, Rattlesnake to Bessemer. In a scant 1 mile the war zone is entered. At

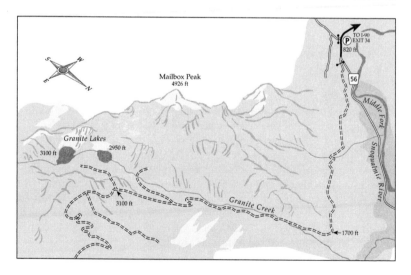

Granite Lake

2½ miles, 1700 feet, the road-trail levels to traverse a cliff and rounds a corner into—at last—the Granite Creek valley. In a scant ¼ mile the way crosses Granite Creek and turns uphill along its course, climbing as steeply as the waterfalls are falling.

At 3100 feet, 2 miles from the turn into Granite Creek valley, is yet another Y. Take the right, crossing two bridgeless (but sure could use them) creeks. If camping is your aim, here is the spot. The boulder field that was a logging road descends. Watch for paths to the lower Granite Lake, 2950 feet, 5 miles from the gate. For the upper lake at 3100 feet, bushwhack up the creek.

An ancient trail route obliterated by logging can be puzzled out on cat tracks to a 4300-foot saddle, 6½ miles from the gate, and the edge of living ancient forest. Look down to Thompson Lake, 3680 feet, logger-free, wheelfree. It's a cinch from there on living trail to Mt. Defiance and the Boy Scout Lakes.

As for "the horror, the horror," it turned out to have a bright side. Those of us who knew the Snoqualmie Pass Highway well had been wailing many a bitter year at the ruthless checkerboard clearcutting. We were dismissed as whining birdwatchers, our proposals for socially responsible logging shrugged off as economically ignorant. The millions of Americans hurtling along "Main Street" scarcely could catch glimpses of what was going on, what with maintaining freeway speed. But when the saws got up into Granite Creek, eyes did not have to be taken off the road. This was in-your-face clearcutting at its most brutal. The muck-a-mucks of the forest industry slowly came to realize that no matter how many millions they spent on four-color magazine ads showing off the beauties of clearcuts, the American voting public was as ignorant as the birdwatchers. When the detailed history of the Mountains-to-Sound Greenway is unraveled, a chapter will be devoted to the important educational role of "the horror, the horror" of Granite Creek.

15 | STEGOSAURUS BUTTE

Round trip: About 4 miles
Hiking time: Allow about 3 hours
High point: 2040 feet
Elevation gain: 1070 feet
Hikable: April–November
Map: Green Trails No. 174 Mount Si

A trail (when one exists, which it doesn't now) up Stegosaurus Butte (which has a humped back and bristling trees along the spine, just as shown in your kid's dinosaur book) might well become the most popular picnic-walk in the Middle Fork Snoqualmie valley. However, we advise you to wait. Just now it is only a proposal, and not one lacking critics.

From Exit 34 on I-90, pick up the Middle Fork Road (Hike 13, Mailbox Peak) and follow it 11.8 miles to the Gateway Bridge parking area, elevation 1000 feet. The butte stands on high directly across the Gateway Bridge.

In season the local NIMBY grumps resent the intrusion of bushwhackers on the huckleberry banquets. But they don't eat views: south to the valley of Rainy Creek, north to Mt. Price and Preacher Mountain, down to the glacier trough of the Middle Fork, and beyond it to the dumbfounding 4000-foot south face of 5519-foot Mt. Garfield, which wouldn't have to apologize were it in Yosemite Valley.

Given a favorable environmental impact statement that gives due

Limited view from Stegosaurus Butte

consideration to NIMBY rights, Forest Service approval, and the hardhat volunteers to donate sweat, the brush might be made to yield a family trail. By sacrificing a very few trees on the 2040-foot summit, the window could be opened wide to the massive granite wall of Garfield. Toddler-safe railings at the brink would permit the picnic to proceed.

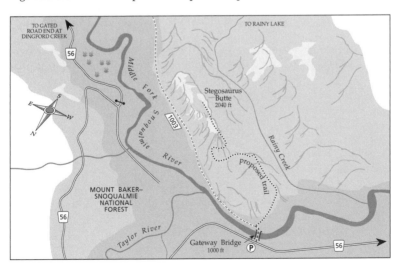

16 MIDDLE FORK SNOQUALMIE RIVER: DOWNSTREAM FROM GATEWAY BRIDGE TO RAINY CREEK POOL

Round trip: 1½ miles
Hiking time: Allow 1 hour
High point: 1000 feet
Elevation gain: None
Hikable: March–November
Maps: Green Trails No. 174 Mount Si, No. 175 Skykomish

The trails here have been abandoned since Pearl Harbor. The nation had urgent business abroad and, when done, airplanes assumed most responsibility for patrolling the forest. Walking for the sheer joy of it was pretty much lost in the shuffle. Some logs must be crawled over, sections of tread are missing, and the brush has never quit growing. But the moss has built a soft cushion for the boots, solitude deepens at every windfall, and the relict handiwork of the 1930s trail crews, when big logs were sawn through by misery whip, not chainsaw, makes the scene sort of a history museum.

The Forest Service intends a reconstruction in which the Middle Fork trail will become a star attraction of the valley. Plans are in progress for a major addition to the Alpine Lakes Wilderness from the Middle Fork up the Pratt River. When all trails are in place, the now almost vacant Gateway parking lot will be full. At present the downstream stretch of the Middle Fork trail to Rainy Creek Pool is very hikable.

From Exit 34 on I-90 pick up the Middle Fork River road (Hike 13, Mailbox Peak) and follow it 11.8 miles to the Gateway trailhead, elevation 1000 feet.

Cross the Gateway Bridge and turn right, descending momentarily to the river level. For ¾ mile the way alternates between mossy forest floor

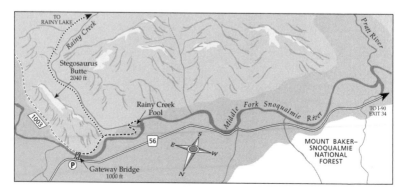

and sky-open gravel bars, ending abruptly at a deep, swirling pool beneath a flawless cliff. Here is where the family has its picnic, tosses pebbles in the pool, maybe takes off shoes and cools the feet. Be careful; the pool is deep.

Beyond here, the route disintegrates.

About halfway between the trailhead and Rainy Creek Pool, just past the base of Stegosaurus Butte, an unmarked but readily spotted trail, unmaintained but well-beaten by the boots of hungry fishermen, takes off up Rainy Creek to forest-ringed Rainy Lake, 3764 feet.

Middle Fork Snoqualmie River

17 | MIDDLE FORK SNOQUALMIE RIVER: UPSTREAM FROM GATEWAY BRIDGE

Round trip: 6 miles
Hiking time: Allow 3 hours
High point: 1100 feet
Elevation gain: 300 feet
Hikable: Almost all year
Maps: Green Trails No. 174 Mount Si, No. 175 Skykomish

Within the memory of folks who until recently were still nimbly ambling (or stiffly creaking) about the backcountry, a hiker who was setting out up the Middle Fork had to hoist pack practically at North Bend. Then "lokie loggers" entered the valley with rails and spent a dozen-odd years clearcutting the floor of the glacial trough (and of Pratt River as well), climbing the valley walls as far as a high-line cable could reach to skid logs to a landing, and incidentally obliterating the trail. In the 1930s the CCC Truck Road was built by one of the New Deal's best ideas, the Civilian Conservation Corps. In the 1960s a valley-bottom road was built along the old logging-railroad grade to replace the CCC Road, and in the 1980s the Forest Service began planning to restore a walking route in the lower valley, leading to the never-extinguished one in the upper valley. Located across the river from the noise and dust of the modern road, green and peaceful in second-growth forest getting more old-growth-like each passing decade, the trail will provide the all-year walking that has been scandalously rare in "the center ring, the big business, the heart of the Snoqualmie matter."

Though blue-sky visionaries dream of a trailhead at North Bend (or, rather, a connection there to a Sound-to-Mountains trailhead on saltwater of the Whulge), plans actually on the drawing board are for a trail from the Pratt River to Dutch Miller Gap. The 7½ miles from Gateway to Goldmeyer

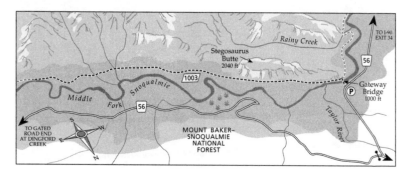

Gateway Bridge and Mt. Garfield

Hot Springs and the 12 miles from there to Dutch Miller are open and walkable but lie beyond the scope of this book. However, the quiet side of the river cries out for at least a look-see. Hike 16 suggests one downstream from Gateway. Following is one upstream.

Drive the Middle Fork Road (Hike 13, Mailbox Peak) 11.8 miles from I-90 to Gateway trailhead, elevation 1000 feet.

Cross the architectural marvel of Gateway Bridge, built in 1993, and turn upstream. The first few hundred feet of trail are the most beautiful, squeezed between river and cliffs. Across the Middle Fork is the confluence with the Taylor River.

The trail turns inland and climbs away from the river, at ¾ mile passing under the noble granite wall of Stegosaurus Butte; when the sun is out, it shines almost as bright. Mudholes appear and the trail is forced to detour around a slide area. At about 1¾ miles the way follows the old logging-railroad grade. At 3 miles the trail descends to the river level, an appropriate turnaround for the look-see.

18 LAKE BLETHEN–ROOSTER MOUNTAIN

Round trip: 10 miles
Hiking time: Allow 7 hours
High point: 3198 feet
Elevation gain: 2000 feet
Hikable: May–mid-November
Map: Green Trails No. 174 Mount Si

Ira says Lake Blethen is a charming forest lake encircled by big cedars and cliffs. However, don't ask me for a recommendation, because the last time I was in that part of the country, loggers were rooting out the huckleberry bushes to ship overseas and four-wheelers were yahooing through the stumps assassinating beer cans. However, a degree of civility is being restored, and there's nothing to get in the way of the scenery—you can say that for clearcutting. As for the lake, I avoid those at this elevation because they are infested with people, but then, that's me. Ira likes the lake (any lake). They photograph well and in the pictures you can't see the mosquitoes.

From Exit 34 on I-90, drive the Middle Fork Road 12.3 miles to the Taylor River, cross, and turn left for 0.4 mile. Park near the second Taylor River bridge (firmly gated), elevation 1100 feet.

Walk Taylor River road-trail ⅓ mile to a Y. Up right is the Taylor, up left Quartz Creek. The road-trail steeply ascends the narrow Quartz valley

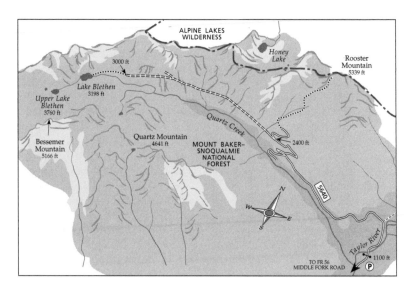

some 2 miles. The valley then widens, as do the clearcuts, which climb to 4000 feet or even, on nearby Bessemer Mountain, to 5000, and only quit when the mountain does.

At 3 miles the grade is washed out. About ½ mile beyond, keep left at an obscure Y. At 4 miles, 3000 feet, the road-trail dwindles to naught and a path beaten by feet finishes the ½ mile to Lake Blethen, 3198 feet.

No doubt the fisherfeet have proceeded another and very steep ½ mile to another and smaller hole in the ground filled with water, Upper Lake Blethen, 3760 feet.

My recommendation is to forget the lakes. Instead, go off right on a sideroad-trail at about 2 miles, 2400 feet or so, and follow it toward the 5339-foot summit of "Rooster Mountain."

Mount Garfield from Quartz Creek road

19 TAYLOR RIVER: OTTER FALLS, LIPSY LAKE, AND BIG CREEK FALLS

Round trip to Lipsy Lake: 8½ miles
Hiking time: Allow 4 hours
High point: 1750 feet
Elevation gain: 650 feet
Hikable: March–November
Maps: Green Trails No. 174 Mount Si, No. 175 Skykomish

Old maps show a "Lake Dorothy Highway," a shortcut from Seattle to Stevens Pass via the Taylor River, Snoqualmie Lake, and Miller River. After World War II major steps were taken toward implementing the plan; roads were built up the Miller to within 2 miles of Lake Dorothy and up the Taylor to within 2 miles of Snoqualmie Lake. One would suppose that the establishment of the Alpine Lakes Wilderness would have put the quietus to the highwaymen's pipe dream, but as late as 1999 public officials were speaking of it as a plan still afloat. (Note the sign at the split in the Middle Fork Road pointing to Lake Dorothy!)

We don't think so. The loggers having long since gone away, their Taylor River road is mellowing into a delightful foot trail through green shadows of new forest. The river tumbles close below. Peaks of Garfield soar

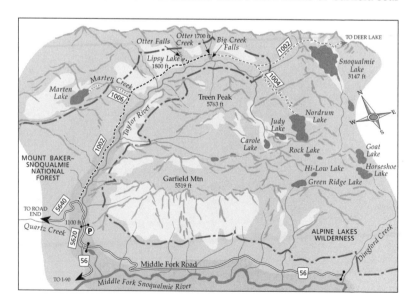

sharply high. The varied thrush trills, the winter wren twitters. The forest floor is carpeted with deer fern, elkhorn moss, teaberry, and bunchberry. Massive granite blocks invite scrambling.

Drive the Middle Fork Road to the Taylor River (Hike 16, Middle Fork Snoqualmie River: Downstream from Gateway Bridge to Rainy Creek Pool). Cross the Taylor bridge and turn left 0.4 mile to the gate at the second bridge, elevation 1100 feet.

Walk the Taylor River road-trail ⅓ mile to a Y. Where Quartz Creek goes left, go right. The tributary creeks are the stars of the show, which is why the trip is best taken from late April to early June when the creeks are flushing winter down to the sea.

At 3 miles is the first of the big waters, Marten Creek, the falls churning a pool of limeade. A mean little old trail 100 feet short of the plank bridge climbs to awesome ancient cedars, some more than 12 feet in diameter.

Beyond Marten, several loud creeks tumble through culverts. There is also a rockslide that must be carefully crossed, and jackstraw jumbles of

Otter Falls and Lipsy Lake

avalanched logs where passage has been made possible by a lot of chainsawing. At 1¼ miles from Marten is Otter Creek, flowing through a particularly large culvert. Several hundred feet beyond, find a distinct though unsigned trail. That's the way to go. Ira and Pat started up too soon and left bits of torn shirts and pants and quantities of blood in a thicket of slide alder. As for me, I never did find the trail, which climbs 100 feet and drops to Lipsy Lake.

Lipsy Lake! What's *that* all about? Whatever; Ira shot a ton of film of the gem of a pool below a 500-foot granite slab down which Otter Creek plunges in one waterfall after another.

Beyond Otter Creek ¾ mile is Big Creek, 1700 feet, crossed by a massive concrete bridge. (Why *here*? For that shortcut highway?) Snow-water sheets down smooth granite, by far the finest otter slide of all. I lingered long at lunch, waiting, but they never showed up.

For a person wanting more exercise, Snoqualmie Lake is a couple of long, steep miles away at 3147 feet in the Alpine Lakes Wilderness. It's a lake, so you know there will not be solitude.

20 | MYRTLE LAKE–HESTER LAKE

Round trip to Myrtle Lake: 14 miles
Hiking time: Allow 7 hours
High point: 3777 feet
Elevation gain: 2400 feet

Round trip to Hester Lake: 12 miles
Hiking time: Allow 7 hours
High point: 3886 feet
Elevation gain: 2500 feet
Hikable: July–October
Map: Green Trails No. 175 Skykomish

A good chance to be actually lonesome? Have the lakes been poisoned by fanatics determined to expel finny interlopers from ecosystems that Nature didn't intend for them? No, but it's a brave or reckless or wealthy fisherman who joyously risks tens of thousands of dollars worth of machinery in the 6 miles of misery from the Taylor River to Dingford Creek. The violence of Nature and the poverty of the Forest Service will combine to end attempts to keep the old road passable to any machine less powerful than a D-6 caterpillar tractor. Indeed, beginning probably in 2003 the road will be gated shut from November to April to protect the winter-soft road from destruction by ordinary wheels.

Lake Dorothy from pass above Myrtle Lake

Drive the Middle Fork Road to the Taylor River (Hike 19, Taylor River: Otter Falls, Lipsy Lake, and Big Creek Falls). Punish your car (or walk) 6 miles to Dingford Creek trailhead, elevation 1400 feet.

The badly eroded trail switchbacks steeply 1 mile up second-growth forest dating from railroad-logging of the 1920s–1930s. The Alpine Lake Wilderness

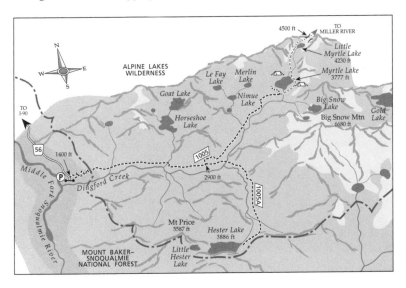

Myrtle Lake

is then entered, the forest cool and virgin, the grade easier, and the roar of close-by Dingford Creek is soothing music to your ears. At 2900 feet, about 3⅓ miles, the trail splits.

The left fork is to Myrtle Lake. A short switchback and a long upvalley traverse ascend moderately through rough patches and mudholes to the lake, 7 miles, 3777 feet. For views of Big Snow Mountain, take the boot-beaten path left around the south shore.

Boots can go where clouds can go. Turn right, over the outlet. The trail shrinks to a path and then, like the Cheshire cat, vanishes altogether in knee-deep brush and knee-bruising windfall. Cross Myrtle's inlet stream to the west side (the USGS incorrectly shows the trail staying on the east side) and proceed upvalley. The trail, magically reappearing, and quite good though unmaintained, switchbacks steeply, passes waterfalls, and at 1 mile from the cirque of Big Myrtle levels off in the upper cirque of Little Myrtle Lake, 4230 feet. The once-upon-a-time-built trail ends in ½ mile at a 4500-foot pass leading to the Miller River.

For Hester Lake, at the 3⅓-mile junction at 2900 feet, take the right fork. The trail is in poor condition and will be allowed to stay that way for people wanting a chance to get away from people. The rude path crosses Dingford Creek, then ascends, moderately at first, in subalpine meadow-marshes and patches of trees, before heading straight uphill to Hester Lake, 6 miles, 3886 feet. The deep blue waters are set in a cirque gouged from 5587-foot Mt. Price; impressive cliffs rise from the shore.

You say there still are too many people for your delicate sensibilities? You yearn for pure solitude? It's all around you. For a starter, fill your water-bag, escape the tyranny of lakes and creeks, and camp in the vicinity of that pass to the Miller River. Run the vacant ridges to your heart's content.

21 | ROCK CREEK–SNOW LAKE

Round trip from Dingford Creek: 15 miles
Hiking time: Allow 9 hours
High point: 4100 feet
Elevation gain: 2800 feet
Hikable: Mid-July–September
Map: Green Trails No. 207 Snoqualmie Pass

Since the Cascade Crest Trail moved to Gold Creek to become the Pacific Crest Trail, this portion of the old route has gotten so lonesome that half the tread is soft moss. To be sure, the brush has grown up too; a ½-mile stretch may be real misery and some of the rockslides are less than pleasant. But you'll have Rock Creek to keep you company, 1200 vertical feet of

Rock Creek Wall from Rock Creek trail

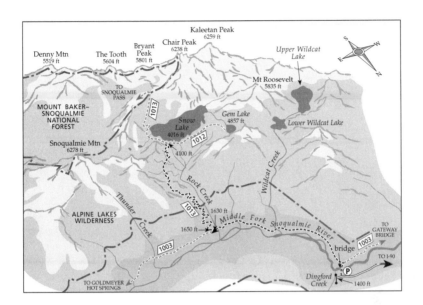

cascades and falls spilling from Snow Lake, and no people to keep you company until the lake. Compared to the approach from Snoqualmie Pass used by the masses, this is 5½ miles longer and gains 1100 feet more elevation. Worth it.

Drive to Dingford Creek trailhead (Hike 20, Myrtle Lake–Hester Lake), elevation 1400 feet. Or not. If the road to Dingford Creek is impassable, start at Gateway Bridge (Hike 16, Middle Fork Snoqualmie River: Downstream from Gateway Bridge to Rainy Creek Pool), adding 6½ miles each way.

Drop to the river, cross, and hike upstream on the Middle Fork trail 2 miles to Rock Creek. At a junction just beyond, elevation 1630 feet, turn right, uphill, on trail No. 1013, paralleling Rock Creek. After leveling off on an old railroad grade, at 2½ miles, 1650 feet, the trail turns uphill again.

At 3½ miles are views out the Middle Fork to Yosemite-like granite walls of Mt. Garfield. At 4½ miles leave second growth for virgin forest. At 5½ miles look out windows to the Rock Creek headwall and a superb waterfall. At 6 miles is a miserable brush-covered rockslide, ending at 6½ miles when the way clambers over a rock rib to meet the Snow Lake trail, 7½ miles, 4100 feet. The lake is a short walk in either direction; turn right for the smaller mobs.

Olallie Lake

SOUTH FORK SNOQUALMIE RIVER: NORTH RIDGE

The South Fork Snoqualmie carries the "Main Street of the Northwest," corridor of electricity, electronic buzz (Elite Mail, FAX, and, yes, the semi-archaic telephone), natural gas, liquid petroleum fuels (ever just a faulty valve and a lighted cigarette away from incinerating innocent civilians), and a googol of thunderwagons and Terminator trucks. Yet on any given day the corridor is populated by more feet in motion for pure fun than all the in-line and skateboard and scooter runs in the Northwest. Interestingly enough, not to toot our own horn too loud, more than half the trailheads between the North Bend Plain and the outskirts of Snoqualmie Pass have been known to the general hiking public only since we began our guidebooking in the mid-1960s.

The high points of Snoqualmie Pass have, of course, been almost super-popular since The Mountaineers built their Snoqualmie Lodge in 1914 and drew up two lists, ten each, of Snoqualmie Lodge Pin Peaks. Well into the 1950s, earning the two "Snoqualmie Pins" was a milepost on the journey to the "Six Majors Pin" and, after that, who could say? Everest was not climbed until 1953.

To the west of the Pin Peaks lay a whole other realm. I daresay that for every climber who ever has stood atop a Snoqualmie Pass summit, a thousand male lads have strangled on the smoke of wet wood at camps on shores of the "Boy Scout Lakes," otherwise frequented only by the breed of fishermen who will drop a hook in any rainwater puddle that looks like it might harbor a hatchery trout.

The eventual addition of the bathing suit to the mandatory gear of a Boy Scout was an acknowledgment that females had quit fainting, as formerly was thought fundamental to their delicate nature, and begun sweating. It also became apparent that the "Closer Is Better" rule required much more intensive recreational exploitation of the South Fork. Thus began our guidebook advertising of more trails than e'er were known to lake-doting Boy Scout or fisherman.

The exploitation of the South Fork has not quite been maximized, nor should it ever be. The portion of the North Ridge in the Alpine Lakes

Wilderness will have to be more and more carefully protected against the crush of too much love. The Wilderness's wilderness must be forever wild; in the words of Thoreau, "In wildness is the preservation of the world," which we of today interpret to be a recognition that though civilization is the triumphant creation of city man, when lacking easy access to the non-city, man goes mad mad mad and there goes your world.

The Alpine Lakes Wilderness must be enlarged at certain necessary points. However, much of the North Ridge is and will remain outside, and properly so, because most of it rates no better than a 5 or 6 on a wilderness scale of 10. But a 5 or 6, or 4 or 3, is far superior to 1 or 2, and is ample to give a degree of spiritual balm; more people seeking balm can be served by more low-impact (low-speed, low-decibel) wildland-edge trails.

Let us not, though, automatically consider every new trail an enlargement of Heaven. Other creatures were living in this wildland before man arrived—and still are, when we let them—and they must be allowed their space. The Issaquah Alps Trails Club began its campaign to preserve certain wildlands by building trails as political broadsides, trails to stir the feet of voters, which bears and deer are not. In the Alps, having gained at the polls victory over wheels, we sat down with public land managers to write plans for the recreation of people afoot—and for the survival of resident wildlanders afoot and a-wing and a-fin and (snakes) a-belly. We deconstructed certain of our "political" trails to give the wildlife their refuge from our feet. We declared that no new trails should be built without consent and encouragement by the proper agency, be it King County Parks, State Parks, or state Department of Natural Resources.

I go to such lengths because some of us long have been suggesting a new walking route, a North Ridge Trail from Mailbox Peak to Granite Mountain. A practical way could be surveyed, no doubt about that; I know walkers who have done the distance. Hikes that can be hooked together for looping purposes, combinations of Mailbox, Dirty Harry, Bandera, and Granite, would be aesthetically delightful and joys to the long-leggity. So let's think about it, but not rush into anything. Interview the wild residents. Inventory their getaway places.

22 | DIRTY HARRY'S BALCONY

Round trip: 5 miles
Hiking time: Allow 4 hours
High point: 2613 feet
Elevation gain: 1300 feet
Hikable: February–December
Map: Green Trails No. 206 Bandera

My great regret is missing out (several times by mere minutes) on meeting Harry Gault, the Quintessential Gypo, a Vanishing American, who necessarily must vanish, but still. . . .

The first I heard of him, in 1977, was an unimproved road shown on a State Highway Department engineer's map, labeled "Dirty Harry's Logging Road." This struck me as a gratuitous slur by a public agency, but not so—"Dirty Harry" was what he liked to be called by his North Bend friends, who were legion, looking on him as their local (sort of) Paul Bunyan. For many years his business and pleasure was purchasing cutting rights to timber on private land that didn't interest the big operators and chainsawing scraggly, next-to-worthless forests to desolation, practicing logging methods subsequently outlawed, thanks in no small part to the horrors he committed in full view of the millions of travelers on the Main Street of the Northwest. He was the despair of the Forest Service and Weyerhaeuser, which tried in vain to shunt him off to out-of-the-way places where he wouldn't give the timber industry such a flagrant black eye.

Driving I-90 along the South Fork Snoqualmie upvalley from the moraine, a person paying attention to more than concrete and machines notes that at a certain point the valley, quite wide upstream and downstream, is constricted by a ridge thrusting from the side of Defiance Ridge. A person with an eye for rock may look up and judge this a most impressive collection of precipices and chimneys. If that person has a taste for pedestrian exercise, he/she may wonder what

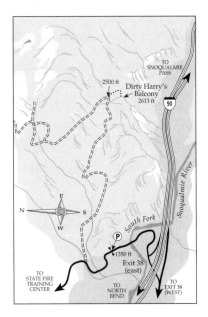

South Fork Snoqualmie River from Dirty Harry's Balcony

it's like to be up there on top. Well, he/she ought to go find out. Ought to
look down from bald buttresses, down and down more than 1000 exceed-
ingly vertical feet, to a most impressive collection of concrete ribbons and
busy machines. But the view down is only a fraction of the vista from Dirty
Harry's Balcony. Furthermore, in season the rock garden is a brilliance of
blossoming herbs and shrubs.

Coming from the west, go off I-90 on the west entry to Exit 38 and drive
old US 10, now a rest-and-recreation boulevard that ends at a freeway underpass that is the east entry to Exit 38. Follow signs, "State Fire Training
Center," 0.2 mile north of the underpass to a gate, signed "Locked after 4
p.m. Road ends 2.5 miles ahead." At 0.2 mile from the gate (which is the
most dependable all-hours trailhead) is a bridge over the South Fork Snoqualmie.

At ⅓ mile from the bridge is the gravel lane to the left that for a time led to a
timber bridge over the river, Dirty Harry's connection to old US 10. In ¹⁄₁₀ mile
more, on a curve and easy to miss, Dirty Harry's Logging Road, unsigned,
climbs to the right. Just a trail now. And creekbed. Elevation 1350 feet.

In 1½ miles, at 2500 feet, Dirty Harry's Logging Road switchbacks west.
Go off right on a path to a saddle between Defiance Ridge and Balcony
Ridge. Just past the saddle turn right and follow the path ½ mile through

snags of a silver forest, shrubs, and salal onto the mossy, craggy bald top of Dirty Harry's Balcony, 2613 feet.

Zounds! Look east to Bandera, south to McClellan Butte, west to Mt. Washington, and—from other viewpoints nearby—farther west to Rattlesnake, the lower Snoqualmie valley, and the Olympics. But especially look down the giddy crags to the concrete swath of I-90, where bugs chase each other's tails east and west, and to the gravel channels of the river, and to the abandoned railroad grade and the gashes of tree-mining roads that climb so high, almost touch the sky, and would be hauling logs from there, too, if Nature could grow trees on clouds and if Congress had legislated a Northern Pacific Cloud Grant.

From the first bald top explore others, stepping very gingerly along the brink, admiring airy pillars and deep-incised chimneys and scary cliffs. In spring the knobs and pillars and chimneys and cliffs are a glowing garden of penstemon and paintbrush and beargrass and much more.

23 | DIRTY HARRY'S PEAK

Round trip: 11 miles
Hiking time: Allow 9 hours
High point: 4650 feet
Elevation gain: 3400 feet
Hikable: May–November
Map: Green Trails No. 206 Bandera

Harry Gault's crazy road and scandalous logging were familiar sights from old US 10 for years, but when at length I tried to get there, his timber bridge over the river was gone. My first entry, therefore, in 1977, was from the North Bend Plain, up the moraine via the 1883 Seattle–Walla Walla Toll Road. At the top of Grouse Ridge I was boggled by the spectacular scene unseen and unsuspected from the highway—a gravel mine that has been nominated (by me) as the hugest in the Free World, and probably the Evil Empire and the Third World as well. The day still had some juice in it when I reached the far end of the mine and picked up the crazy road shown on the State Highway Department engineer's map. Up and up it went, all boulders and waterfalls, and how Harry ever got trucks up and down is beyond mortal imagination.

The peak demanded to be climbed and to do so took all the juice remaining in my day and my legs. Coming down, dreading a long, miserable tramp by flashlight, I discovered that the new lanes of I-90 bridged the river and, though not open to traffic, could be scampered across with relatively little risk of capture and imprisonment. The shades of night were

McClellan Butte from Dirty Harry's Road-Trail

falling fast as I pessimistically stuck out my thumb; a kindly trucker screeched to a stop and whisked me back to square one.

Now, of course, the State Fire Training Center has opened wide the Dirty Harry Country. So, go off I-90 as directed for Hike 22, Dirty Harry's Balcony, to the start of Dirty Harry's Logging Road, elevation 1350 feet.

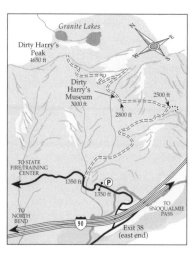

In 1½ miles, at 2500 feet, where the path goes off right to the Balcony, the road-trail switchbacks left. Continue west 1¾ miles to a promontory at 2800 feet, far enough for snowline-probing in early spring. When Harry went away the alders began growing up thick as hairs on a dog's back. However, in 1999 I got a phone call from a Lone Volunteer who has adopted the road-trail and on solo work parties whacks alders and even reconstructs tread. He could use help. The views, mainly through windows he has opened, are across the valley to McClellan Butte, down to I-90 and river, east to Snoqualmie Pass peaks, and out the portals of the Cascade front to the lowlands.

At 3000 feet the road crosses a tumbling creek, site of Dirty Harry's Museum, trucks and machines scavenged from junkyards and kicked and cussed up here for a final rusting place. At about 4000 feet the alder begin to thin out and windows open wider. At about 1½ miles from Museum Creek, the road tops out on the very summit of the 4650-foot peak of Defiance Ridge that I have named (and let the Board of Geographic Names take note) for Harry.

Count rings in the stumps of trees that when he chainsawed them down were little more than a foot in diameter. The counting is difficult, the rings are so close. Most of the trees were rotten at the core; Harry hauled perhaps one in five to the mill. One wonders where he found a mill that would bother with mountain hemlock.

Turn to the views. West beyond the final two peaks of Defiance Ridge (Peak 4926 and 4841-foot Mailbox) are North Bend, Rattlesnake Mountain, Issaquah Alps, smog-dimmed towers of Seattle, the smoke pall of invisible Tacoma, Green Mountain (the one just west of Bremerton), and the Olympics. South, beyond Mt. Washington, is Rainier. North is Baker. Easterly are Kaleetan, Chair, Chimney, and that other volcano, Glacier Peak. Beyond the Middle Fork are the boggling clearcuts on Bessemer Mountain. Straight down the cliffs (watch your step) are the clearcut shores of Granite Lakes.

24 | MASON LAKE–MOUNT DEFIANCE

Round trip to Mason Lake: 6 miles
Hiking time: Allow 6 hours
High point: 4800 feet
Elevation gain: 2600 feet in, 200 out
Hikable: June–November

Round trip to Mount Defiance: 11 miles
Hiking time: Allow 10 hours
High point: 5584 feet
Elevation gain: 3700 feet in, 200 feet out
Hikable: July–October
Map: Green Trails No. 206 Bandera

Though never an aficionado of the Boy Scout Lakes (our Depression-era troop never could assemble enough fathers' cars to take hikes this deep in the real mountains), came a day when I thought I'd go take a look at one.

Mason Lake is the quickest mountain lake from the city, and I'd heard that fisherfolk had beaten out a trail. My error was looking for it on the wrong side of Mason Creek and, to make a long story short, ending up on top of Mt. Defiance. I finally reached the lake by descending from there. I still couldn't find the trail because the lake basin was deep in snow. So I climbed up and over Bandera Mountain.

On a subsequent trip I found the trail and understood why the Forest Service was trying to discover the identity of the anonymous volunteer "trail builder"—so they could indict him on charges of attempted murder. Such is the fatal attraction of holes in the ground filled with water and stocked with alien fish that the miserable path blazed by the "benefactor" was endangering innocent throngs inveigled by the sign that said "lake." The rangers attempted to obliterate the ill-made trail, but more hardhat saints continued to keep up the treacherous trail.

At last the rangers agreed with me that Mason Creek was not the way to go; my route over Bandera Mountain was. In 2002 and 2003 VOW (Volunteers of Washington), working under close Forest Service supervision, put in a new route up and over Bandera.

Go off I-90 on Exit 45, signed "Forest Service road 9030." At a split in 1 mile, go straight ahead on road No. 9031, signed "Mason Lake Way." At 3.8 miles from the freeway, the road is blocked. Park here, elevation 2200 feet.

Ascend the abandoned road, now trail, pass Mason Creek, and in a scant 2 miles from the parking area reach the end of the 1950s logging road. Here begins the new-built "official" trail that has replaced the bulldozer spur roads and 1958 fireline that Buddy Pal and I found in the 1960s. Switchbacks ascend in post-fire forest of young trees, then pretty shrubs

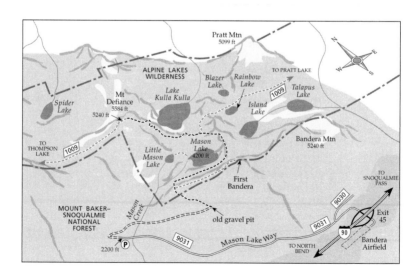

and picturesque bleached snags. In ½ mile, near the 4800-foot ridge of Bandera Mountain, the trail splits. The right is to the summit, the left switchbacks down to intersect the trail between Mason and Island lakes.

As a destination, Mason Lake is—generously—a C minus. Mt. Defiance, now, there's another story. Definitely A-plus. Mountain meadows, the closest of such high quality to Seattle. Enormous views.

Ascend the ridge trail west on south slopes of Defiance ½ mile to a junction between Mason Lake and Lake Kulla Kulla. At 5240 feet, about 2 miles from the junction, a meadow is a glory of blossoms in early summer. A steep scramble up the west edge culminates in the summit, 5584 feet.

Gaze. Over the Middle Fork Snoqualmie to Baker and Glacier. Over the South Fork to Rainier and Adams and, on a smogfree day, what's left of St. Helens. Five volcanoes, that's a lot.

Trail above Mason Lake on side of Mount Defiance

25 | BANDERA MOUNTAIN

Round trip: 7 miles
Hiking time: Allow 6 hours
High point to best view: 5050 feet
Elevation gain: 2850 feet
Hikable: May–October
Map: Green Trails No. 206 Bandera

I was on my way home from a missionary trip to Utah the day the 1958 firestorm blew up. In the mid-1960s, accompanied by my five-year-old Buddy Pal, Claudia, and our sheepdog with the piebald eyes, Natasha, I scrambled to the margin of the 1958 burn and clambered over dozens of charcoaled logs. (Said sad but wise Buddy Pal, "Daddy, you don't get no place 'sploring.") Only on the descent did I find the fireline trail whacked along the edge of the burn by the Smokey Bears.

From the last black log, the way continued upward in beargrass and silver snags of nineteenth-century blazes. (After some 150 years, there is not so much as the start of a new forest, vivid testimony to the scientific fact that logging at this elevation is not "tree-farming" but "timber-mining.") Mountain-wise Buddy Pal looked to a lichen-gray granite talus and confidently announced, "Marmots live there." Daddy said, "Well, maybe conies." Conies did indeed squeak. But a marmot whistled too. Score one for the kid.

Drive road No. 9031 (Hike 24, Mason Lake–Mount Defiance) to the barricade, elevation 2200 feet.

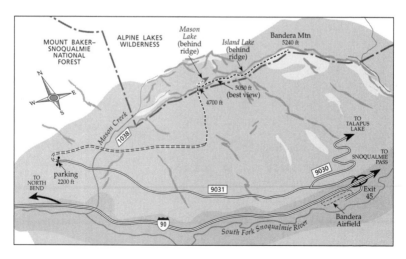

Follow the Mason Lake (Hike 24) trail past Mason Creek to the end of the road-trail, a scant 2 miles from the parking area. Go left on a true trail and head for the sky, first in young trees, picturesque bleached snags, and, then, in season, fields of beargrass.

The trail nears the ridge at about 4700 feet directly above Mason Lake. The trail-split to the left is to Mason Lake (Hike 24). Go right, climbing east on the ridge crest through subalpine trees and scramble granite blocks up a ridge step to the first summit of Bandera Mountain, 5050 feet. The views here are as good as they get; most hikers will not bother with the down-and-up on a wooded ridge to the highest summit, 5240 feet. You don't get

I-90 from Bandera Mountain

no pin for this mountain. Look down to lakes in forest bowls, out north to Glacier Peak and Baker, northeasterly to Snoqualmie peaks, down south to the freeway and beyond to Rainier, and west past the portals of Mt. Washington and Mailbox Peak to Puget Sound. Civilization is near but so is wilderness.

26 | TALAPUS AND OLALLIE LAKES

Round trip: 4 miles
Hiking time: Allow 3 hours
High point: 3780 feet
Elevation gain: 1220 feet
Hikable: June–October
Map: Green Trails No. 206 Bandera

A well-groomed forest trail, perfect for first-time backpackers and families with young hikers, leads to two popular lakes and gives access to many more, the area crisscrossed by trails providing infinite opportunity for exploration. Due to the proximity of Puget Sound City, a weekly average of 425 hikers visit here throughout June, July, and August, mostly on weekends.

Go off I-90 on Exit 45, signed "Forest Road 9030," cross under the freeway, and continue straight ahead west 1 mile on road No. 9030 to a split. Go right, uphill, still on road No. 9030, for 5.4 miles to the end at Talapus Lake trail No. 1039, elevation 2650 feet.

The trail begins on an overgrown logging road through an old clearcut, enters forest shade, and in several gentle switchbacks and a long sidehill swing reaches a marshy area just below Talapus Lake. Paths here branch in several directions. The muddy track stays on the north side of the lake's

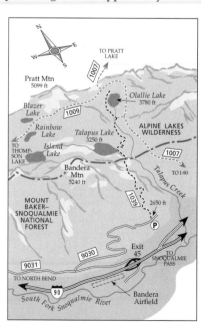

Talapus Lake

outlet stream. The main trail crosses the outlet on a bridge and at 1¼ miles comes to Talapus Lake, 3250 feet.

The way continues, ascending over a rib ½ mile to meet the sidetrail down from the Pratt Lake trail; turn left ¼ mile to Olallie Lake, 3780 feet, completely wooded.

(To proceed farther, ascend either by the sidetrail or directly from the far end of Olallie Lake to the Pratt Lake trail. Meadows and views start immediately.)

27 | PRATT LAKE SADDLE

Round trip to saddle above lake: 11½ miles
Hiking time: Allow 8 hours
High point: 4100 feet
Elevation gain: 2300 feet in, 700 feet out
Hikable: July–October
Maps: Green Trails No. 206 Bandera, No. 207 Snoqualmie
Pass

Miles of deep forest and a lovely lake amid subalpine trees. A network of trails leads to other lakes and to meadow ridges and high views.

Go off I-90 on Exit 47, signed "Denny Creek," cross over the freeway, and turn west 0.4 mile to the trailhead parking area, elevation 1800 feet.

The first steep mile gains 800 feet in cool forest to a split. The Granite Mountain trail goes right; stay straight ahead, pass a nice creek, and sidehill upward on gentler grade in young forest, through patches of twinflower, Canadian dogwood, salal, and bracken, by many nurse logs, to Lookout Point, 3 miles, 3400 feet.

At 3¾ miles is a short sidepath down to Talapus and Olallie Lakes. The main trail rounds the Olallie basin in open subalpine forest to a 4100-foot saddle, 4 miles, a logical turnaround point for day-hikers. Lots of huckleberries here in season, plus a view south to Rainier, and a junction with the Mt. Defiance trail. The Pratt Lake trail switchbacks down a steep hillside of

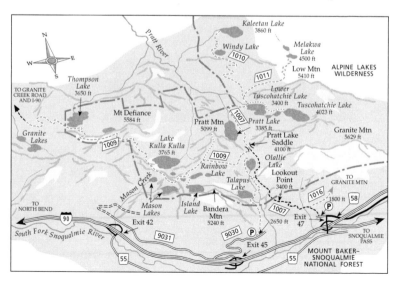

much mud, some covered with puncheon, flattens out and contours above the lake, then drops to the outlet, 5¾ miles, 3400 feet.

Now for explorations. On trail No. 1007, a scant ½ mile from Pratt Lake, is Lower Tuscohatchie Lake, 3400 feet, and a choice of three directions for wandering: A fishermen's path beats brush 1½ miles to Upper Tuscohatchie Lake, 4023 feet. From the outlet of Tuscohatchie Lake (Lower), a less-used trail climbs northward to 4800 feet and drops past little Windy Lake to Kaleetan Lake, 3860 feet, 3½ miles. The way is entirely in forest with only occasional views over the Pratt River valley, logged in the 1930s, but the lonesome lake has a splendid backdrop in the cliffs of Kaleetan Peak.

From the Pratt Lake Saddle (see above), Mt. Defiance trail No. 1009 ascends westward through beargrass and berry meadows (fine views 1100 feet down to Talapus Lake) on the side of Pratt Mountain, whose 5099-foot summit is an easy scramble via huge boulder fields on the southwest side; passes Rainbow Lake (Island Lake lies ½ mile away on a sidepath and actually is a more rewarding objective than Pratt Lake); comes near Mason Lake; traverses high above Lake Kulla Kulla; and climbs past flower gardens almost to the summit of 5584-foot Defiance, about 3 miles. The trail continues westward on the ridge a mile, drops to Thompson Lake, 3650 feet, 5½ miles, climbs to a saddle, and descends a maze of logging roads through a vast clearcut to the Granite Lakes.

Pratt Lake saddle

28 | GRANITE MOUNTAIN

Round trip: 8 miles
Hiking time: Allow 8 hours
High point: 5629 feet
Elevation gain: 3800 feet
Hikable: July–October
Map: Green Trails No. 207 Snoqualmie Pass

The most popular summit trail in the Snoqualmie region, for good reason. Though the ascent is long and in midsummer can be blistering hot, the upper slopes are a delight of granite and flowers, and the panorama includes Rainier south, Baker and Glacier Peak north, Chimney Rock and Mt. Stuart east, and googols of other peaks, valleys, and lakes.

The mountain is lovely—and it's a killer. In spring its sunny southwest shoulder melts free of snow very early, seeming to provide bare-trail access to the heights. But the trail doesn't stay on the shoulder; it crosses a gully where snow lingers late and where climax avalanches thunder nearly to the edge of the freeway, sometimes carrying the bodies of hikers who should have chosen Bandera Mountain instead.

Go off I-90 on Exit 47, signed "Denny Creek," to the north side of the freeway, and turn west 0.4 mile to the Pratt Lake–Granite Mountain trailhead parking lot, elevation 1800 feet.

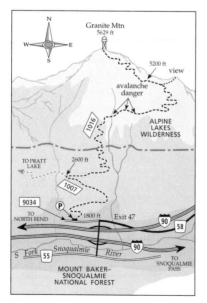

The first steep mile on the Pratt Lake trail gains 800 feet in cool forest to a split at 2600 feet; the creek here may be the last water.

Go right from the split, traversing in trees ½ mile, then heading straight up and up in countless short switchbacks on an open south slope where fires and avalanches have inhibited the growth of forest. (On sunny days start early to beat the heat.)

At 4000 feet the trail abruptly gentles and swings east across the avalanche gully—an area of potentially extreme danger sometimes through June. Hikers seeking the summit before July should be very wary of crossing this gully; better to be content with the already very

Crystal and Upper Tuscohatchie Lakes from Granite Mountain trail

nice views to the south over the Snoqualmie valley to Rainier.

Beyond the gully the trail sidehills through rock gardens, passing a waterfall (early summer only) from snows above, and then switchbacks steeply to grass and flowers, reaching the summit ridge at 5200 feet. In early summer the route beyond here may be too snowy for some tastes; if so, wander easterly on the crest for splendid views over the Snoqualmie Pass peaks, down to alpine lakes, and through the pass to Lake Keechelus.

The trail ascends westward in meadows, above cozy cirque-scoop benches, and switchbacks to the fire lookout, 5629 feet, 4 miles.

29 | DENNY CREEK SLIPPERY SLAB

Round trip: 2½ miles
Hiking time: Allow an entire hot afternoon
High point: 2800 feet
Elevation gain: 500 feet
Hikable: May–October
Map: Green Trails No. 207 Snoqualmie Pass

Denny Creek is the happiest valley of the Snoqualmie Pass vicinity, one waterfall after another fluming and splashing. Were an election held to choose the best, the pre-teen vote would be a landslide, and the kindergarten–nursery school bloc unanimous, for the famous Slippery Slab.

Go off I-90 on Exit 47, signed "Denny Creek," cross over the freeway to Denny Creek road, turn right (east), passing under the freeway, and continue 3 miles to Denny Creek Campground. Just past it, turn left on a road over the river and follow it 0.2 mile, passing private homes, to the road-end parking area and trailhead, elevation 2300 feet.

Walk watchfully to avoid head-on collisions—there is no centerline painted on the trail, which ascends moderately along Denny Creek in forest, passing under the high bridge of I-90 (keep an eye out for falling trucks), crossing the stream on a bridge at ½ mile and recrossing at 1¼ miles, 2700 feet, below water-smoothed slabs of a lovely cataract.

The slabs! O the slippity-sliding! O the ice-cold water! O the hot sun that de-blues the skin! Except in snowmelt flood-time, the creek sheeting over the slabs is never deep enough to endanger a slider, and the granite is so smoothed by long action of the creek, and the sliders' bottoms are so

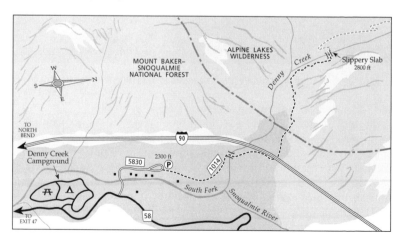

cushioned by the tumbling water, that never is a bottom bruised. At the end of each slide is a plunge basin—ice water in your eye, young shriekers!

A major problem may be shooshing away teenagers who try to hog the sport; adults should firmly exile them up the trail to Keekwulee Falls, 1½ miles, and the ensuing 1 mile of tight switchbacks around cliffs past Snowshoe Falls (Hike 30, Melakwa Lake).

To herd little kids past the Slippery Slab to more distant destinations simply can't be done. Parents are advised to relax, take off boots, and cool at least their feet if not their bottoms.

Denny Creek Slippery Slab

30 | MELAKWA LAKE

Round trip: 9 miles
Hiking time: Allow 6 hours
High point: 4909 feet
Elevation gain: 2600 feet in, 350 feet out
Hikable: Mid-July–October
Map: Green Trails No. 207 Snoqualmie Pass

The reader may have noticed that I, no fisherman (though some of my best friends . . .), am less than absolutely uncritical of lakes, as such. Granted, they tend in the higher elevations to be located amid some of the grandest scenery the glaciers have wrought. Also, thanks to the fish that people have planted (there were none in the high lakes primevally), they almost always are accessible by trail, and you can't say as much for holes in the ground that are not filled with water.

Having so stated my reservations about the genus lake, I must straightforwardly confess that I adore Melakwa Lake. Why? The way the meadows shelve so neatly into the water? The meadows ain't what they used to be, nor will be again until boots quit making mudpies. The way Chair Peak's cliffs leap from one side and Kaleetan's flowers and talus rise gracefully from the other—or, in proper season, the snowfields that give such a whoop-de-doo glissade from the Kaleetan summit? Or is it a matter of memories, good times over many years?

Anyway, I put my money on Melakwa Lake as the crown jewel of Snoqualmie Pass.

Drive to the Denny Creek trailhead (Hike 29, Denny Creek Slippery Slab), elevation 2300 feet. The trail climbs to the Slippery Slab at 1¼ mile,

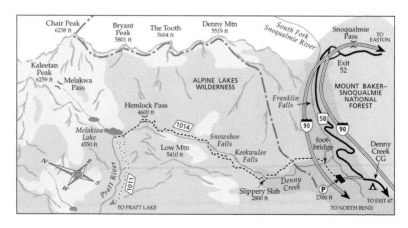

Melakwa Lake

2800 feet, leaves forest, and strikes upward in avalanche greenery to Keekwulee Falls, 1½ miles, and switchbacks around cliffs past Snowshoe Falls at a scant 2 miles. At 2 long miles, 3500 feet, the path flattens out in the upper basin, shortly crosses the creek, goes from trees to avalanche brush to trees again, and switchbacks to wooded Hemlock Pass, 3½ miles, 4600 feet. From here the trail drops a bit in forest to the outlet of Melakwa Lake, 4½ miles, 4550 feet.

Turn around here if you must. If time allows, continue around the meadow shore to the inlet, thence to the head of the basin and the low pass and over it to—well, not to give away all the secrets, this is my favorite spot in the Snoqualmie Pass area. It also is the connoisseur's route to Snow Lake. Check your map.

31 | FRANKLIN FALLS

Round trip: 2 miles
Hiking time: Allow 2 hours
High point: 2600 feet
Elevation gain: 200 feet
Hikable: Mid-June–November
Map: Green Trails No. 207 Snoqualmie Pass

The Snoqualmie Pass area's most watery-exciting, history-fascinating, ancient-forested, family-style walk. Joan Burton, in *Best Hikes with Children in Western Washington and the Cascades*, says, "A paradise for kids! Standing beside the 70-foot falls on a warm day, they scream with joy at the cold spray in their face." But that's not the half of it. The beautiful moss-covered forest has grand old trees. Traces remain of prospect holes that were expected to disgorge riches to establish the Pittsburgh of the West. A stretch of corduroy road dates from the 1860s–1870s. The Snoqualmie Pass Wagon Road lives on after a century and a third. I vividly recall when this was our family route to the Mysterious East; children who suppose I-90 was the Lord's creation on the eighth day goggle at the rude track and accuse us of putting them on, say it was impossible ever to have an America with highways like this.

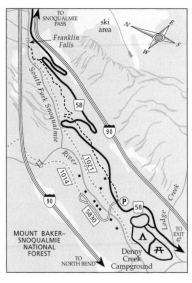

Roadside sign

Drive I-90 to Exit 47, signed "Denny Creek." Cross to the north side of the freeway and turn right on Denny Creek road, pass under the freeway, and stay left. At 3 miles pass Denny Creek Campground.

A bit farther, a verifiable remnant of the Snoqualmie Pass Wagon Road starts a 1-mile climb to Franklin Falls; turn left and park this side of the Denny Creek bridge. From the parking area either follow the old wagon road or the forest trail; they unite in ¼ mile. Both ways are well marked and easy to follow. The old Sunset Highway zigzags up to the pass, offering shortcuts. Not to be confused with the old, old wagon road. Shortcuts are fine but they miss the beautiful old moss-covered forest.

Whether you get there by trail, Wagon Road, or shortcuts, the last 200 feet to the falls are steep; small children will need a helping hand.

The falls is spectacular and so is the high bridge of I-90 high above; an amusing (sort of) bit of history here. This is the second high bridge the highwaymen built. Mountaineers who knew the site gave warning but the engineers sneered and went ahead. The first winter the bridge was in place, it was overwhelmed and half-wrecked by a climax avalanche. Fortunately the highway was not yet open. At enormous expense the bridge was rebuilt, enough higher to let the snow slide under.

Franklin Falls

Snoqualmie Valley from Mount Washington

SOUTH FORK SNOQUALMIE RIVER: SOUTH RIDGE

In the past two decades the Issaquah Alps have provided hundreds of new miles of pedestrian paths, the richest trove of near-city wildland walking in the region, perhaps the nation. In that period, on the eastward extension of the Alps, the South Ridge of the South Fork Snoqualmie, comparatively little happened, nor had for a century.

Blame (I certainly do) the Northern Pacific Land Grant, declared by a Congressional investigating committee of the 1920s to be the most monstrous theft from the public domain in the history of the nation. However, the short shrift given foot exercise is the least heinous aspect of that crime.

My generation has numbly watched the year-by-year cut-and-get-out logging of our good green home hills. The experience has been as shocking, staggering, terrifying, infuriating as it was for our parents' generation to witness the rich soils of the prairies blow away, darken the skies of New York and Washington City, the Dust Bowl reaping the whirlwind sown by years of careless farming.

I have listened to the bitter complaints of old hiking buddies who went to forestry school because they loved the forests, were hired by timber companies, and learned that the only "forestry" they were permitted was dictated by the corporate bottom line. Gifford Pinchot's maxim that forests must be managed for "the greatest good of the greatest number in the long run" has properly been dismissed as philosophical gibberish. However, though the words don't make sense, the spirit behind them does, and those who have lived by that spirit throughout their careers know the difference between what Pinchot meant to say and what the bottom-liner CEOs are saying in the board rooms: "The greatest profits for the smallest number and *right now.*"

It will not go on because it must not go on. So, what next for the South Ridge? Man requires wood fiber for his civilization and Nature can and will supply a steady flow of trees—if assisted by men and women who demand to be more than "logging engineers," who are allowed to serve as educated, conscientious "forest ecologists." Their management will be for *genuine* sustained yield of *genuine* multiple uses. The South Ridge, transferred by one means or another back to public ownership, can emulate the management by the state Department of Natural Resources on the Tiger Mountain State Forest, "a working forest in an urban environment." For the South Ridge this will be amended to "a working forest in a social environment," meaning it will provide recreation, re-creation, wildlife habitat, pure water, and all the other social goods a forest offers aside from wood fiber.

To say the South Ridge has not given the feet much new to do in this century is pretty much but not entirely true. The Milwaukee line, after all, has been there since early in the century, and for generations the iron horses and feet got along very well. Indeed, I much preferred walking the rail-trail when the only wheels were iron. They provided welcome entertainment and I was glad to stand aside and watch the thrilling show ("the big wheel runs by steam, the little wheel runs by the grace of God"). Few other walkers shared my solitary pleasure. But they are there now and the Iron Horse Trail must be ranked among the better things done for wildland travelers in recent time.

Nevertheless, I don't consider it the definition of happiness for feet. For wheels, for hooves, yes. But for walkers the greatness of the Iron Horse will be not in what it is but in what it can lead to: at each of those thirteen major creeks in its 21 miles, a picnic spot, a nature trail to waterfalls; the network of logging roads intersected, most fated to be abandoned, some perhaps converted to view roads for family automobiles, others zoned as bombing runs for fat-tire crash-and-burn, others as quiet paths for the horse and boot. Whether or not a high-line South Ridge Trail ever is ultimately judged economically practical and ecologically proper, other trails than those of Annette Lake, McClellan Butte, and Mt. Washington can lead off and up through new-growing forest to big-view summits.

32 | IRON HORSE (JOHN WAYNE) TRAIL

One-way from Rattlesnake to Cascade Crest: 21 miles
Hiking time: Allow 16 hours
High point: 2400 feet
Elevation gain: 1500 feet
Hikable: West end, all year; east end, March–November

Round trip to Washington Creek: 6 miles
Hiking time: Allow 4 hours
High point: 1100 feet
Elevation gain: 130 feet
Hikable: All year

Round trip to west portal of Cascade Tunnel: 5½ miles
Hiking time: Allow 4 hours
High point: 2400 feet
Elevation gain: 200 feet
Hikable: March–November
Maps: North Bend Ranger District and Green Trails No. 206
Bandera, No. 207 Snoqualmie Pass

The Iron Horse Trail ain't what it was cracked up to be when first proposed. True, freight trains no longer disquiet the mountainside forest serenity; instead, deported to the freeway in the valley below, they toss family cars about like tumbleweeds in a dust devil. True, rails and ties no longer trip careless feet and hooves; those impediments, as well as the tall trees that so closely hedged the railroad as to make it a virtual tunnel through the forest, have been removed from a 40-foot wide road, wide enough for a truck, and a 230kw power line. (That buzz you hear on rainy days is not bees.)

So it's not really a "trail" at all, in the ancient and honorable definition. It's a "multi-use travelway." Among the "multis" are service trucks that

Snoqualmie Pass tunnel

require a hard-surface road to let wheels go fast (and make the feet go flat).

Another multi unexpected by the dreamers of old is the newfangled knobby-tired "mountain" bike. A fun machine, to be sure, with no big noise, no poisonous fumes, no depletion of fossil fuels. We appreciate the aggravation of a biker trying to keep the wheels upright while wobbling along at the slow pace of legs. Nevertheless, we must speak up about the difficulty of having a nice day afoot while bikers zip by your ear. At the same time, we sympathize with the biker who, while negotiating clumps of chummy walkers, can't get up to a speed that washes his or her face with a 20-knot wind.

The answer is (ultimately) to separate the swifter (bikers, runners, skaters, truckers) from the slower (walkers, wheelchairs, horses).

Lane separation, however, is only needed where traffic is heavy. For most of these 21 miles, hikers will not be much tempted by the naked swath where lightning buzzes in the wires overhead. Their destinations of choice will be the creeks, nigh onto a dozen major tumbles and countless trickles. Good intermediate accesses to the Iron Horse are Olallie State Park (walk

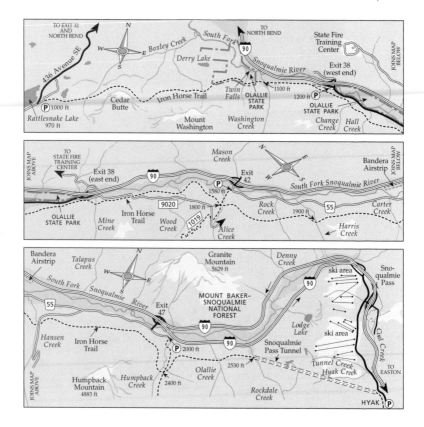

west to Washington Creek, east to Change and Hall Creeks), and McClellan Butte trail (walk east to Alice, Rock, Carter, and Hansen Creeks).

The two ends, though, are the pedestrian favorites, the west end because low elevation keeps it open all year, and the east end because homesickness for our troglodyte ancestry draws us to holes in the ground.

For the west end, go off I-90 on Exit 32, turn south on 436 Avenue SE (Cedar Falls Road) to Rattlesnake Lake, elevation 970 feet. Until the State Park officially opens a trailhead here, use the temporary alternative. At ¼ mile short of the lake, go left on a wide gravel road. Park at the sharp bend. To the right spot the barbwire fence along the watershed boundary, elevation 1000 feet. The trail follows the fence, skirting Christmas Lake to the powerline access road, which ascends to the Iron Horse Trail at about 1 mile east of the eventual permanent trailhead.

The trail crosses Boxley Creek, rounds the slopes of Cedar Butte, and in

Humpback Creek bridge on Iron Goat Trail

three miles comes to the trestle over Washington Creek, 1100 feet, and grand views across the valley to Mount Si. And so home.

For the east end, go off I-90 on Exit 47, turn right 0.1 mile, then left on road No. 55 for 0.6 mile to the Annette Lake trailhead, elevation 2000 feet. The trail crosses Humpback Creek and at 1¼ miles, 2400 feet, intersects the Iron Horse. At 2¾ miles, 2530 feet is the west portal of the tunnel beneath the Cascade Crest. The east portal is 2¼ mile at Hyak. Check your flashlight batteries. Beware of things that go bump.

33 | TWIN FALLS

Round trip: 2½ miles
Hiking time: Allow 2 hours
High point: 1000 feet
Elevation gain: 500 feet
Hikable: All year
Maps: Green Trails No. 206 Bandera, No. 206s
Mt. Washington

The geological story: The glacier descending the Middle Fork Snoqualmie was larger and more powerful than that down the South Fork. The smaller glacier couldn't cut as fast as the larger and, in melting away, left a "hanging trough." When the river broke through the huge moraine (Grouse Ridge) of the subsequent Canadian ice sheet, it quickly hung up on hard rock, forming "Upper Snoqualmie Falls" or "Twin Falls."

Twin Falls Natural Area is famed for the most scenic and toddler-friendliest path along the I-90 corridor, the perfect year-round spot to show visitors

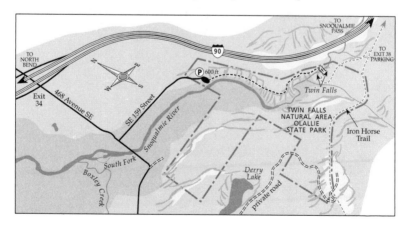

from afar a typical Northwest magnificence of forests and waters. The trail passes through moss-covered and fern-hung trees, a cathedral of ancient forest beside a murmuring river, then ascends to a thundering climax at a footbridge spanning canyon and falls. These recreation amenities were the "amelioration" the developers were required to provide in exchange for their free use of public waters in a public park. The hydroelectric development at Twin Falls is completely underground, invisible to the walker's eye, a supposed model of non-harmful "small hydro." However, though terms of the permit require some water always to be held from diversion into the underground pipe, in the "tourist months" after the melting of winter snows, the spectacle becomes pitiable compared to the old. Visitors from Boston never will see what we locals used to.

Go off I-90 on Exit 34, signed "468 Avenue." From the interchange, turn right (south) on 468 Avenue SE 0.5 mile. Just before the river crossing, go left on SE 159 Street, signed for the state park, originally named "Twin Falls," renamed "Olallie." In 0.5 mile are the road-end parking area, toilets, and trailhead, elevation 600 feet.

Upper Twin Falls

The trail start is a toddlers' delight, through sky gardens of moss in groves of vine maple, superb old, second growth, and fern-carpeted forest, and by riverbars that invite pebble-tossing, stick-floating, picnicking, wading, and watching dippers and kingfishers. The hillside steepens—keep tight hold on a toddler's hand as the trail descends to a grove of even bigger trees; don't miss the 8-foot-diameter spruce on the left and the 9-foot-diameter fir on the right.

From this grove the way climbs within earshot of trucks on I-90 to meet the stairway down to Lower Falls Overlook, an aerial perch with a dramatic view. A few more minutes up the trail is *the bridge!* Stand in midspan a hundred feet above the pools between upper and lower falls. Feel the earth tremble (in snowmelt time, that is). Wonder how the two huge laminated wooden beams were placed here. (Answer: very carefully, by helicopter.)

A hundred yards up from the bridge is Upper Falls Overlook, a good turnaround. To go onward is to soon reach the Iron Horse Trail; turn left and watch for the path angling down to Exit 38 and the upper trailhead.

34 | MOUNT WASHINGTON: OWL HIKE SPOT

Round trip: 4 miles
Hiking time: Allow 3 hours
High point: 2800 feet
Elevation gain: 1600 feet
Hikable: March–November
Maps: Green Trails No. 206 Bandera, No. 206s
    Mt. Washington

I first began eyeing Mt. Washington in the 1960s, boggled by the steady ascent of logging roads to the very summit, intrigued by what surely had to be some of the most enormous views from the Cascade front over the lowlands to Seattle. Desperately wanting to include them in a sequel to our initial *100 Hikes*, I spotted an obscure little road off old US 10, but every attempt to scoot my Volkswagen beetle into the narrow slot was frustrated by a truck riding my rear bumper. Then came I-90 and the little road vanished. The unfinished business was ever on my mind, but so was a lot of other stuff. Late in 1985, voila!—a published description of how to get to the "Owl Hike Spot," a trail trip I'd seen regularly listed in *The Mountaineer* bulletin without knowing what or where it was. Off I went, up and up until my Shelties were shivering in the belly-deep (theirs) snow. As the memory of the sun was extinguished on the western horizon, we descended to warmer climes.

Frozen waterfall on Mount Washington trail

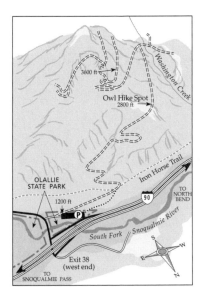

Coming from the west, go off I-90 on Exit 38. Go right on old US 10 a short distance, then right again to the large parking lot for the Twin Falls segment of Olallie State Park, elevation 1200 feet. (If driving west, from the east end of Exit 38 follow old US 10, now a recreation road, 2 miles downvalley to the parking lot.)

Near the restrooms, head up a steepish trail to a road and walk it a short bit to the Iron Horse Trail. Turn right a few hundred feet to an unsigned but well-graveled path leading to what the old map calls a "jeep trail."

Actually it's a gypo logging road of the 1950s or so. In mind's eye see Dirty Harry's decrepit truck, the outside edge overhanging a cliff, Harry at the wheel singing "Nearer My God to Thee." A clever little road-trail it is, picking a devious and ingenious way under and over and between cliffs, gaining elevation steadily and steeply, switchbacking east three times and west three times, finally traversing westward toward the objective. The way is largely in young alder but partly in virgin hemlock with several groves of ancient Douglas fir snagtops (beware the golden eagles). The cliffs are great fun, plummeting below, beetling above—some overhanging, forming impressive caves (beware the jaws that bite, the claws that scratch). Springs gush from crevices and nourish hangings of maidenhair fern and saxifrages. In season the icicles are dazzling. In other seasons there is a sideshow of "sport climbers" dangling from bolts and belts and ropes.

The way is obvious—passing several rude paths (more bolts) to a major intersection at 1¾ miles. Traverse right ¼ mile, around a cliff corner into the broad valley of Washington Creek. Here, at 2800 feet, the Owl Hikers used to cook supper, watch the sun go down and city lights go on, and descend by flashlight. The panorama was a three-star gasper, from Rattlesnake over the North Bend lakebed (South and Middle Forks meandering along either side, freeway slicing through the middle, towns of North Bend and Snoqualmie sprawling) to Little and Big Si and Teneriffe, out the Snoqualmie Falls notch to lowlands and Olympics—and straight down precipices to the gorge of Twin Falls.

Of course, that was then. Trees grow up and leaf out. But the gasper remains, though not much at the Spot anymore. Keep going another mile or so on the route to Mt. Washington (Hike 35) and at 3600 feet or so outclimb the young trees.

35 | MOUNT WASHINGTON: THE SUMMIT

Round trip: 12 miles
Hiking time: Allow 8 hours
High point: 4800 feet
Elevation gain: 3400 feet
Hikable: May–October
Maps: Green Trails No. 206 Bandera, No. 206s
Mt. Washington

As the era of high adventure neared its end in the alpine wilderness of the Cascades and Olympics, there began an "in-filling" of lesser spaces that offered opportunities for originality in an era of low adventure. The University of Washington Night Climbers boldly ascended campus summits, atop one building leaving a suit of red long johns, transformed by headlines in the student newspaper into a "Cossack jacket," a brazen insolence of the

Communist Party. The Blobbers (who transformed the Issaquah Blobs to Issaquah Alps), sortied into winter-rainy brush of the foothills seeking "things to climb when mountains aren't worth it."

When loggers finished shaving the forests from US 10 to the top of Mt. Washington, the summit demanded the boots of every adventurer of spirit who passed by on the way to Snoqualmie Pass. The construction of I-90 and the relegation of a stretch of US 10 to status as a recreation byway solved the problem that caused my own ignominious defeat and brought a swarm of low adventurers to the scene. Ira and I accepted our responsibility to "guidebook" the ascent. However, we had many other responsibilities. Mark Twain in his *Innocents Abroad* tells how he was kept so busy with scientific duties on the Riffelalp, boiling the thermometer and barometer to determine the elevation, that he despatched his trusty assistant to fulfill another tourist duty, the ascent of the Matterhorn. Ira despatched his trusty daughter, Vicky, and husband, Tom, to do Washington for us. Their report follows:

From the trailhead at Olallie State Park (Hike 34), 1200 feet, hike 2 miles to the Owl Hike Spot, 2800 feet. Continue on the logging road to a split at ⅛ mile past the Owl Hike Spot. The peak you seek lies straight ahead, but unless you have an unquenchable lust for brush, go left on a rough trail that switchbacks up the tangled hillside farther and farther from the objective at every step. Another split is passed at 2½ miles from the trailhead; stay right. In ¼ mile more the old road you have been following meets a much younger one. Go left, heading northeast around the hillside. (Mark the intersection as you leave to avoid missing it on the way down.) Round the hillside on the unused road through a clearcut basin,

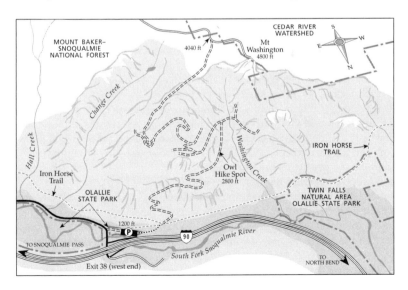

Mount Rainier from Mount Washington

past a spur to the right. At 3¾ miles from the trailhead your road intersects another. Descend it left several strides to a second junction and go right.

The grade mellows, the road quality improves with each junction, as do the views, which open north and east as you enter Change Creek drainage. The road traverses, then skims the crest of a razor-sharp divide, and at 4040 feet, 5¼ miles from the trailhead, attains the forested ridge overlooking the Cedar River watershed. Go left on a grassy road northwest along the crest. In a level ½ mile it divides. Split the difference, go straight ahead on a trail between the two, steeply uphill on the crest to (in season) subalpine color: columbine, tiger lily, "something purple," and the "cow-parsnip-like thing that Mother Pat will identify."

The climb ends at an abandoned metal tower, 4800 feet. Baker, Glacier, and Rainier stand tall in the galaxy of peaks. Chester Morse Reservoir lies below in Seattle's Cedar River Watershed. The full roster of Middle Fork and South Fork peaks spreads out east. To the west only the Olympics block the view all the way to the Pacific Ocean.

There now, wasn't that fun? Somebody owes you a pin.

36 | OLALLIE STATE PARK

Map: Guidebook *North Bend Climbing Rocks Exit 38*

The major attractions of Olallie State Park—Twin Falls Natural Area and the Iron Horse–Mt. Washington trailhead—are described in Hikes 32, 33, 34, and 35. Two other attractions are so minor by comparison they might seem unworthy of mention. Certainly they are not "destinations" sufficient in themselves to justify the ordeal of getting there, driving the battlefield where Terminator trucks go a-hurtling by at 70-plus mph, their swirling eddies lifting little cars from the pavement and whirling them off in the weeds. Yet it is precisely that ordeal that gives major value to the mile-plus stretch of old US 10 bypassed by I-90, reserved for rest and recreation.

While taking the R&R cure for shellshock, the traveler may wish to simply sit by the river and listen to the water. However, other stressfree entertainments may be enjoyed.

WEEKS FALLS
Round trip to falls overlook: ¾ mile
Hiking time: Allow 1 hour
High point: 1200 feet
Elevation gain: None
Hikable: All year

There are two Exits 38 from I-90, a long mile apart; drive the old US 10 from either direction about 0.8 mile to the picnic area, elevation 1200 feet, and find the trailhead on the east side.

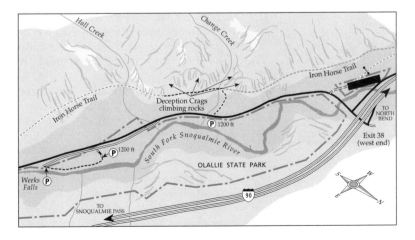

Change Creek climbing wall

The riverside trail passes through a young conifer forest, partly on the route of the Snoqualmie Pass Trail/Wagon Road that was begun, sort of, in 1859, and operated as the Seattle–Walla Walla Toll Road from 1883 to 1892. Note a stretch of cedar puncheon abandoned when the Sunset Highway was opened on a different route in 1915. Spot a bit of moss-covered trail. When was it built? By whom? When abandoned? Wade in the river pools, skip stones.

The trail leads to the hydro works and interpretive display praising the benevolence of the stockholders who preempted a public park and river and put them to work earning dividends.

DECEPTION CRAGS OUTDOOR CLIMBING WALL

Round trip: ½ mile
Hiking time: Allow 1 hour
High point: 1450 feet
Elevation gain: 250 feet
Hikable: April–November

The two favorite spots in Seattle for what we used to call "bouldering" were Monitor (now Schurman) Rock in Camp Long, funded by the Works Progress Administration and built by Clark Schurman in the 1930s, and an exceptionally large glacial erratic, "Glacier Boulder," or, after it was surrounded by new homes of the Wedgewood subdivision in 1947 and we were expelled from the granite, "Wedgewood Rock."

Our urban bouldering of winter months was succeeded in early spring by finger exercises on Little Si, Mt. Erie, Tumwater Canyon walls, Peshastin Pinnacles, and the like, yielding then to the genuine climbing season on real mountains. Reflecting the influence, presumably, of the Colorado boulderers, the Yosemite Vulgarians, the Gunkers of the Northeast, and others, it came to pass that people (mostly new to our area and to mountains) were "doing" the Canyon and the Pinnacles *in summer!* Not as conditioning for high climbing. There was a whole new thing going on: "sport climbing."

Drive about 0.8 mile from either the west or east Exit 38 on old US 10 to a decaying bridge abutment over Change Creek, artifact of the old Sunset Highway. Park on the west side of the bridge, elevation 1200 feet.

Cross the road, step over the railing, and ascend a steep path up the creek a scant ½ mile, gaining 250 feet, to the Iron Horse Trail. Behold! the Change Creek Wall. People have drilled holes (using battery-powered drills) and driven contraction bolts in every highway-near clifflet from Little Si eastward. A series of guidebooks have been published describing every bolt and handhold, naming every pitch.

Actually, sport climbing is predominantly an indoor sport. The weather is better.

37 | McClellan Butte

Round trip from lower trailhead: 9 miles
Hiking time: Allow 8 hours
High point: 5162 feet
Elevation gain: 3700 feet
Hikable: July–October
Map: Green Trails No. 206 Bandera

From I-90, McClellan Butte's appearance is formidable and, in truth, the final short scramble to the summit can be life-threatening. Furthermore, until early or middle July there may be crossings of steep snow that ought to stop hikers but don't always. However, in late summer the trail can be ascended safely to panoramas west over lowlands to Seattle, Puget Sound, and the Olympics, south over moth-eaten ridges to Rainier, and east over stark clearcuts to Snoqualmie Pass. The recorded history of the area dates from 1853, when Captain George B. McClellan journeyed

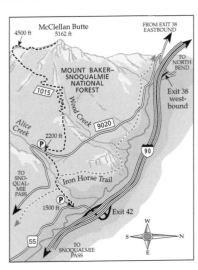

South Fork Snoqualmie River valley from McClellan Butte

approximately this far up the Cedar River valley seeking a pass through the Cascades suitable for the U.S. Army and a railroad.

Drive I-90 to Exit 42, signed "West Tinkham Road," and go right on road No. 55. Cross the Snoqualmie River bridge, pass the highway workshop, and in a scant 0.5 mile turn right to the trailhead parking lot, elevation 1500 feet.

The trail enters forest, climbs a bit, passes under a powerline, crosses the Iron Horse Trail, and at 2200 feet, 1 mile from the trailhead, crosses what used to be and to some extent still is a mainline log-haul road.

Now, about that mainline. It used to be gated at the highway and thus served as a fine footroad, its closure to public machines putting the summit of the Butte that much deeper in trail country. It still can be that deep.

But many folks will take the cheating shortcut and that's bad news. But the good news is that the opening of the road allows an exciting addition to a Sunday Drive.

For Sunday Drivers (devout hikers, shut your eyes), go off I-90 on the west entry to Exit 38 and drive the rest-and-recreation road (old US 10) to the east entry to Exit 38. Turn right onto gravel road No. 9020 (which in some 10 miles comes to the sideroad entry from Exit 47, whose interchange leads across I-90 to Denny Creek Road and thence to Snoqualmie Pass). At a scant 3 miles east from the highway on road No. 9020 is the summit trailhead, 2200 feet. Cheaters start walking here.

The way stays steadily steep, going by a sometime spring in a cool grove of large trees, then switchbacking up the wooded north face of the Butte. At about 2½ miles from the lower parking lot, it rounds the east side of the Butte and crosses an avalanche gully with a treacherous snowbank that usually lasts into July. From here, with numerous switchbacks, the trail sidehills below cliffs in occasional views, attaining the south ridge of the peak at 4 miles, 4500 feet. The crest is followed a short bit, looking down into Seattle's Cedar River Watershed, then the trail rounds the east side of the mountain, drops 100 feet to a small pond, and climbs to a magnificent viewpoint on the ridge crest about 100 vertical feet from the summit.

The majority of hikers are content with the ridge-top view; the summit rocks, easy though they are for an experienced rock climber confident of his/her immortality, are slippery when wet and the exposure is sufficient to be fatal.

38 | MOUNT GARDNER

Round trip to view junction: 3 miles
Hiking time: Allow 2⅓ hours
High point: 3300 feet
Elevation gain: 1000 feet

Round trip to summit: 6 miles
Hiking time: Allow 5 hours
High point: 3800 feet
Elevation gain: 1500 feet
Hikable: March–November
Map: Green Trails No. 206 Bandera

Old maps show a trail from the Snoqualmie valley to the Cedar River, at the high point nearing the summit of Mt. Gardner. How many other trails of the sort never were recorded on maps, golly knows. Finding evidence of their existence would be tough in the stumps and shrub of clearcuts that climb to the edge of the sky, quitting there only because trees wouldn't take root in the clouds. The timber industry has exchanged the stumps for national forest trees. The Forest Service is closing down log-haul roads. The remnants currently provide a rumpus room for big boys with big toys. They, in turn, will eventually go away. What then will the hiker find?

Mt. Gardner calls the curious. The call is not urgent, not as loud as that from trails across the Snoqualmie valley. All the better for a chance of solitude and, except in hunting season, peace. The panorama from Si to Snoqualmie Pass is the more esthetically striking for the contrast with clearcuts, decaying logging roads and bulldozer tracks, powerlines, and the interstate freeway, Main Street of the Northwest, that from sea to sea never sleeps.

Driving I-90 from the west, go off on Exit 39 (the western one) to old US 10, now a rest-and-recreation byway. In a scant 2 miles, just before (the eastern) Exit 39 from I-90, turn right on road No. 9020. At 0.3 mile is (perhaps) a mud wallow that before August may threaten to swallow family cars whole, children and picnic baskets and all. In 1 mile the road crosses the Iron Horse Trail, at 2.6 miles passes the McClellan Butte trail, and at about 3 miles crosses Alice Creek. The way, until now reasonable, turns rude and at 6.1 miles turns steeply upward. Here the family car will chicken out. Plenty of room to park and give the car some peace, elevation 2350 feet.

Afoot, the steepness is a cinch. At ½ mile is a switchback. In 1 long mile begins a talus field large enough to catch the eye from I-90. At 1½ miles, 3300 feet, is a junction that demands an extended soaking-up of the scenery while feasting on peanut butter sandwiches.

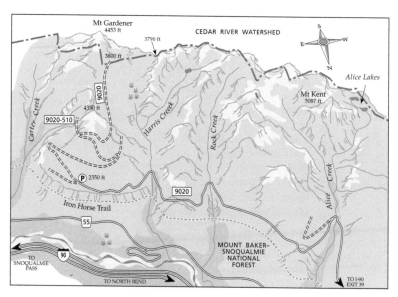

Looking down valley from side of Mount Gardner

Far enough? The views beyond are no better, but do get bigger. From the junction the right fork swings around the nose of Gardner ridge into the broad valley of Harris Creek, to not much purpose. Instead, go left on a switchback a scant ½ mile to another junction. Take the switchbacking right fork, sidehilling below the 4350-foot north summit of Gardner, to the boundary of the Cedar River Watershed, 3800 feet, where your feet must legally quit, 3 miles from where your chicken car did.

The 4453-foot main summit of Gardner is ½ mile due south; a bit closer to the southwest is the 3790-foot pass to the Cedar River valley. The most dramatic feature hereabouts is the rugged mass of 5087-foot Mount Kent to the west, standing above cliffs of a nameless ridge, 4703 feet.

39 | ASAHEL CURTIS NATURE TRAIL

Loop trip: ½ mile
Hiking time: Allow 1 hour (this is not a race track)
High point: 2000 feet
Elevation gain: 180 feet
Hikable: Most of the year
Map: Green Trails No. 207 Snoqualmie Pass

An easy step from a hot, noisy freeway into a cool forest of giant trees, some 4 feet in diameter. Look up, up through their interlaced canopies. You almost can see the sky.

Drive I-90 to Asahel Curtis/Denny Creek Exit 47. Coming from the west, turn right 0.2 mile, then left on road No. 5590 another 0.3 mile to a large Annette Lake–Asahel Curtis parking lot, elevation 1900 feet. (If coming from the east, take Exit 47 and cross over the freeway to road No. 55, then go left on road No. 5590 to the parking area.)

Two trails start from the upper end of the parking lot. That to Annette Lake begins on an abandoned road. The nature trail instantly enters cool forest beside Humpback Creek. Actually, it is not quite the forest primeval it appears. Large stumps tell that a few of the best trees were removed seventy or eighty years ago. There is, of course, the roar of the nearby freeway.

Put plugs in your ears (but remove them to listen to the creek). Ignore those mossy stumps. The trees that were a century or more old when their

Bleeding heart

companions fell are getting on now toward a third century. The understory is a carpet of moss, swordferns, deer ferns; tree trunks are draped with licorice ferns. Leaves of the skunk cabbage are huge, blossoms of starflowers delicate. Come with a flower book in hand. Plan to spend at least an hour.

Cool bench on nature trail

40 | ANNETTE LAKE

Round trip: 7¼ miles
Hiking time: Allow 4 hours
High point: 3600 feet
Elevation gain: 1400 feet
Hikable: June–November
Map: Green Trails No. 207 Snoqualmie Pass

A super-popular subalpine lakelet below cliffs and talus of Abiel Peak, ringed by open forest and masses of humanity, much of it very young. For quiet walking, try early summer or late fall in the middle of the week in a storm.

Go off I-90 on Exit 47, turn right 0.2 mile on road No. 55, and turn left on road No. 5590 for 0.3 mile to the parking lot, elevation 1900 feet (Hike 39).

Two trails start from the upper end of the parking lot. Take the righthand trail along an abandoned road in forty-year-old trees, cross Humpback Creek, and in 1 mile pass under a powerline and enter forest. At 1¼ miles, 2400 feet, cross the Iron Horse Trail.

Now comes the hard part, switchbacking steeply upward in nice old forest on the slopes of Silver Peak, occasional talus openings giving looks over the valley to Humpback Mountain. After gaining 1200 feet in 1½ miles, at 3600 feet the way flattens a final mile of minor ups and downs to the lake outlet, 3½ miles, 3600 feet.

Wander the east shore for picnic spots. Study the architecture of the little cliffs. Listen to the waterfall splashing into the lake.

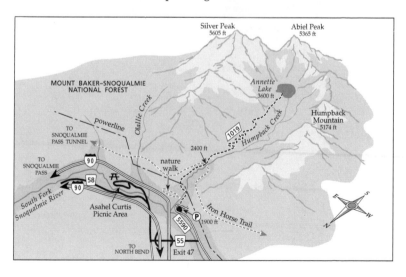

Humpback Creek

41 PROPOSED: SCOUT LAKE–SILVER PEAK LOOP

Loop trip: 15 miles
Hiking time: Allow a lengthy day
High point: 5200 feet
Elevation gain: 3300 feet
Hikable: June–November
Map: Green Trails No. 207 Snoqualmie Pass

Don't try to hike the loop this year—the trail ain't there yet and may never be if our proposal has some flaw we haven't detected. How does the route sit with the wildlife community? Does it impinge on their needs for a retreat from boots boots boots marching up and down again? Does it transform a goodly chunk of rather deepish wilderness to easy-tramping edge wilderness? Whatever; we think the close-to-city I-90 corridor, particularly in the Snoqualmie Pass vicinity, could use some new walking opportunities—assuming such can be found without "damaging the resource," which is to say, taking another crucial bite out of long-suffering Mother Nature.

The sketch map here marks the route we've looked at partly from close-up, partly from a distance. In the counterclockwise direction, from the Annette Lake trailhead (Hike 40), the loop would go west about 1 mile on the Iron Horse Trail. New construction would climb the north side of Humpback Mountain and round the west side to a 4080-foot high point

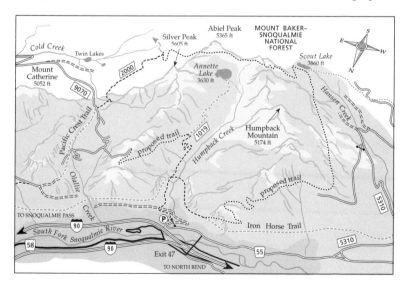

Mount Rainier from Silver Peak

above Scout Lake. From there it would ascend to near the summit of Abiel Peak and follow old tread of an abandoned trail to join the Pacific Crest Trail on the south side of Silver Peak. In about 1½ miles, new construction would descend to the Annette Lake trail, reaching it at a point well down the valley from the lake and thus not adding to the crowds on the shore.

Snow Lake

SNOQUALMIE PASS

'Twas a dark and stormy night of the late 1950s and I was speeding home from weeks of peddling snake oil on the High Plains. Ascending the steeps from Keechelus Reservoir, I was surprised by a glow in the clouds where from time immemorial had been, at this hour in this weather, Stygian blackness. The nearer I approached the pass, the brighter the glow, the more intensely clouds were suffused by unearthly illumination. I was stumbling upon some horrible catastrophe. Should I turn around and flee east? Call the police, the Forest Service, the Red Cross?

The highway flattened at the summit and I saw the catastrophe—constructed since my last crossing of the pass some weeks earlier, a brand-new eight-pump full-service gas station. No cars anywhere, no people in sight. My goggling eyeballs were the only witnesses of an eruption of more electrical incandescence than there was to be seen, that night as from time immemorial, in the whole distance between Cle Elum and North Bend.

When I was a kid our family crossed the pass only in the course of Depression-era flights back and forth across the nation. We never went there for pleasure. If mountains were wanted, we went to The Mountain. To entertain visiting relatives, we took them to Snoqualmie Falls. In later years, when as a student in the Climbing Course I became a regular on the Snoqualmie Pin Peaks, the nights were still so dark, the highway so quiet, that we threw down sleeping bags virtually beside the pavement for a few hours before setting out in the predawn.

Time will not have a stop. A *Seattle Times* editorial of July 16, 1992, put Snoqualmie Pass in perspective:

> *Travelers to or through Snoqualmie Pass are greeted with a panorama that varies moment to moment, mile by mile. Majestic mountain peaks fade into the background as the eye is bombarded, first by downhill ski areas, unlovely sights all but a few months of the year, then by massive clearcuts.*
>
> *More recently roadside developments at the pass—both commercial and residential—have further detracted from the natural grandeur and scenic potential of that unique stretch of interstate highway.*
>
> *Let's face it. Snoqualmie Pass today is, well, tacky. The eastern gateway to the Puget Sound region is a haphazard conglomeration of A-frames and services for travelers and skiers.*

In that third-of-a-century period of population explosion and Eisenhower's

Crusade for Freeways, I experienced another and very similar time-warp. In my rounds as a peddlar, I found myself on a weekend of late autumn handy to Wyoming's Big (Jackson) Hole, and in the evening before a morning ascent of part of a Teton, lay in the sagebrush on the lone prayer-ee to be lullabied asleep by the coyotes crooning. Earlier in the evening I had supper in the town and amid cowboys and ranchers felt expected to explain my out-of-season presence to native eyes met on the street.

Time passed. I returned with wife and kids, memories of the Big Hole kept alive over the years by many viewings of the movie classic retelling the Western Myth. I knew it would be different before we got there, because the 1950s single-lane-with-turnouts "interstate" over the pass from Idaho to the Hole had been replaced by a full-scale Eisenhower. Still, on the main street of the town of Jackson, the Now so harshly contrasting with the Then, I couldn't keep myself from embarrassing my family by shouting, "Shane! *Don't come back!*"

To again quote that editorial in the *Seattle Times,* "The pass could be one of the main focal points of the (I-90) corridor. It could be but it's not. Today Snoqualmie Pass is more a scenic blight than scenic delight."

We defenders of wilderness did our darndest. We insisted that Snoqualmie Pass ski areas should not be allowed to groom every slope for sport, that condos and rathskellers not fill all the valleys. We did manage to save Commonwealth Basin, the last refuge in the pass vicinity for those who seek quiet enjoyment of the natural scene. The Alpine Lakes Wilderness we won commences just there and goes on and on and on to where the deer and the mountain goats play.

42 | COMMONWEALTH BASIN–RED PASS

Round trip to Red Pass: 10 miles
Hiking time: Allow 5 hours
High point: 5350 feet
Elevation gain: 2700 feet in, 250 feet out
Hikable: Mid-July–October
Map: Green Trails No. 207 Snoqualmie Pass

Hikers sorrowed by the half-century civilizing of Snoqualmie Pass tend not to go there anymore. Too much pain. However, diehard veterans of the war to save Commonwealth Basin from yo-yos and yodels suffer the anger for the sake of the triumph—peaceful subalpine forest, rippling creeks, an enclave of "olden days" ideal for a family picnic.

Go off I-90 on Exit 52 at Snoqualmie Pass to the Alpental road and Pacific Crest Trail parking lot, elevation 3000 feet. (Coming from the east, go off on Exit 53.)

The ancient and honorable trail entered the basin in 1 mile, but on private land that ultimately was clearcut, causing the old path to erode so severely it was abandoned. The new way takes 2¾ miles and in the doing gains 700 feet, of which 250 are lost.

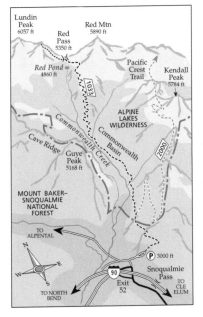

Red Mountain from Commonwealth Basin

Follow the Pacific Crest Trail 2¼ miles, to where it dips near the basin floor before starting up Kendall Peak. Drop on a signed sidepath to the old Commonwealth Basin trail. (Go left or right for picnics.)

The basin trail turns upstream 1 mile to the valley head and ascends the crest of an open-forested spur in many, many short switchbacks. The way flattens in the heather gardens and subalpine trees of a cirque at the foot of Red Mountain. A few steps away on a sidetrail is Red Pond, 4½ miles, 4860 feet. Eat lunch, tour the bouldery and flowery shores, listen for marmots whistling, walk to the edge of the cirque, and look over the valley and the rimming peaks and south to Rainier.

The trail swings up talus and rock buttresses almost but not quite to the ridge crest, then sidehills west to Red Pass, 5 miles, 5350 feet, and views to the deep Middle Fork Snoqualmie valley, the sharp tower of Thompson, the rugged Chimney Rock group, and far horizons.

This used to be the official Cascade Crest Trail and descended from the pass to the Middle Fork Snoqualmie River trail; a doughty soul might do it yet.

Blueberries at Red Pass and Mount Thompson

43 | KENDALL KATWALK

Round trip: 10⅔ miles
Hiking time: Allow 7 hours
High point: 5400 feet
Elevation gain: 2700 feet in, 300 feet out
Hikable: Mid-July–mid-October
Map: Green Trails No. 207 Snoqualmie Pass

The bag of superlatives is quickly exhausted on this, one of the most spectacular stretches of the Pacific Crest Trail in Washington, and among the most accessible and popular.

Go off I-90 on Exit 52 (use Exit 53 from the east) at Snoqualmie Pass to the Alpental road and the Pacific Crest Trail parking lot, elevation 3000 feet.

The trail ascends forest 2 miles, loses 250 feet to negotiate a boulder field, and at 2¾ miles passes the connector to the Commonwealth Basin trail. Flattening briefly, the way switchbacks endlessly upward, at 4300 feet crosses an all-summer creek that may be the last water until Ridge Lake, and at 4700 feet attains the wooded crest of Kendall Ridge. On a long traverse around the mountain, the path opens out in Kendall Gardens, the start of alpine color that is virtually continuous for several hiking days north. At 5⅓ miles a 5400-foot bump is a happy turnaround for a day hike.

To continue involves stepping carefully along the Kendall Katwalk, blasted across a cliff in solid granite. When snowfree it's safe enough. When snowy, forget it. The mountainside moderates to heather meadows. At 6¼ miles is the 5270-foot saddle between tiny Ridge Lake and large Gravel Lake.

The trail passes very near the summit of Alaska Mountain, 7¾ miles,

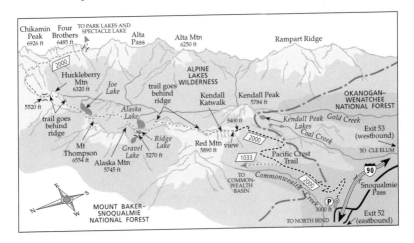

Pacific Crest Trail crossing the Kendall Katwalk

5745 feet, to Huckleberry-Chikamin saddle, 10¼ miles, 5520 feet (due to ups and downs, a gross elevation gain of 1100 feet from Ridge Lake). On the way it swings above the basins of Alaska Lake and Joe Lake, both 1000 feet below and without recommendable sidetrails.

44 | SNOW LAKE

Round trip: 8 miles
Hiking time: Allow 6 hours
High point: 4400 feet
Elevation gain: 1300 feet in, 400 out
Hikable: July–October
Map: Green Trails No. 207 Snoqualmie Pass

Snow Lake is the largest alpine lake (more than a mile long) near Snoqualmie Pass. On one side cliffs rise steeply to Chair Peak and on the other forests fall steeply to the broad, deep gulf of the Middle Fork Snoqualmie

River. The trail and lake are overwhelmingly popular—some 25,000 visitors a year, 800 or more on a fine summer Sunday. If it's the sound of silence you're seeking, be warned.

Go off I-90 on Exit 52 (Exit 53 from the east) at Snoqualmie Pass and drive 2 miles on the Alpental road through the ski area and subdivision to the parking lot and trailhead, elevation 3100 feet.

The trail climbs a bit in forest and then ascends gradually, sometimes in trees, sometimes on open slopes with looks over the 3800-foot droplet of Source Lake (the source of the South Fork Snoqualmie River) to Denny Mountain, now civilized, and to The Tooth and Chair Peak, still wild.

The way swings around the valley head and switchbacks a steep ½ mile in heather and flowers and parkland to the saddle, 3½ miles, 4400 feet, between Source Creek and Snow Lake. Not until here is the Alpine Lakes Wilderness entered. Hikers may well be content with the picnic spots in blossoms and blueberries and splendid views. The trail drops sharply ½ mile to meadow shores of Snow Lake, 4 miles, 4016 feet, and rounds the north side.

More lakes, more private, lie beyond. Walk the shore ½ mile to where the Rock Creek trail plummets to the Middle Fork and a bit more to the creek, the lake's outlet. Cross on a logjam. In 1 mile is Gem Lake, 4800 feet. The path rounds the east shore, climbs a 5000-foot pass, and drops 1000 feet to the two Wildcat Lakes.

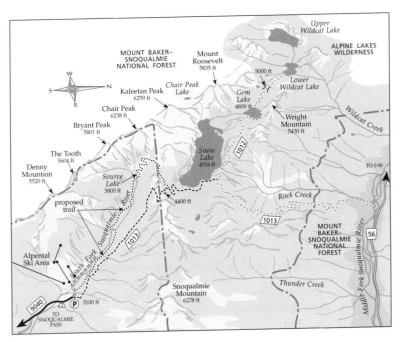

Snow Lake from the saddle

PROPOSED: SNOW LAKE VIEW–SOURCE LAKE LOOP

Inasmuch as the Alpental ski area–vacation home subdivision was permitted by Congress to annex into non-wilderness the valley of Source Creek all the way up to the saddle to Snow Lake, the protections required by the Wilderness Act do not apply to any but the final ½ mile of the Snow Lake trail. As part of the wilderness-defending community, we fought the crimes against Source Creek and Denny Mountain; I mournfully recall a winter day, snowshoeing just where now is a beer hall, when I was stopped dead in my tracks by the sudden flight of an entire large family or village of flying squirrels across an open white plain from one grove of silver fir to another.

But that's a done deal. To take the better with the bitter, the non-wilderness limbo of the Source Creek valley provides an opportunity to drastically reduce the people-encounters a hiker must expect on so busy a trail, and to do so with no fudging of the Wilderness Act—indeed, visitation at Snow Lake, within the Alpine Lakes Wilderness, would be so reduced by this proposal as to considerably enhance the chances of some solitude.

The proposal is to establish a loop route. It would include the existing

Snow Lake trail to the saddle top and a trail junction a few feet within the Alpine Lakes Wilderness (a small fudging price to pay for such benefits). The trail to the right would be signed "Snow Lake," that to the left,"Snow Lake Viewpoint" and "Source Lake Loop." This would follow the old, abandoned Snow Lake trail route to the highest practical viewpoint, contour slopes above and around Source Lake, and return to the parking area.

The viewpoint, almost 400 feet higher than Snow Lake, would become the destination for most hikers. They could, of course continue down to Snow Lake if they wished, but regaining the lost elevation from lake to saddle would be a disincentive; novice hikers could quickly comprehend, resting at the saddle, that a lake always is prettier from a distance.

45 | LODGE LAKE

Round trip: 3 miles
Hiking time: Allow 2 hours
High point: 3500 feet
Elevation gain: 500 feet in, 375 feet out
Hikable: June–November
Map: Green Trails No. 207 Snoqualmie Pass

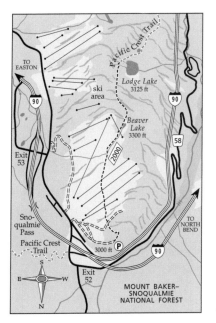

North of Snoqualmie Pass City, the Alpine Lakes Wilderness summons the seeker of peace and green. South of the pass, the sensitive hiker quails at the nakedness of ski slopes and clearcuts. So strongly does the north call and the south repel that—ironically—a person may find more solitude to the south. Much history is there too, to be felt if not seen.

Drive I-90 to Snoqualmie Pass. Coming from the west, go off on Exit 52; from the east, on Exit 53. Follow the frontage road on the south side of the freeway to the west edge of the ski area and continue on a dirt road 0.2 mile to the far end of a large parking area and take off south on the Pacific Crest Trail, elevation 3000 feet.

Walk ¼ mile in forest. Flinch as the trail emerges to groomed slopes of the Summit West Ski Area. On a sunny day, hope for a cloud because the only shade is that of chairlift towers. But the absence of trees does open grand views of the Alpine Lakes Wilderness. From this distance the ski area warming huts, hotels, and restaurants look sort of like a scene from a Swiss Alpine Calendar. Sort of.

Beaver Lake

In ¾ mile the way tops a saddle, the 3500-foot high point of the trip, and gently descends to Beaver Lake (pond, really), 3300 feet, a scant 1 mile from the parking lot. Ira photographed a great blue heron feeding in the lake. The bird took squawking exception to this invasion of privacy and flapped up in the air, circled around, landed on a tree too skinny to hold its weight, fell off, circled around, and, cursing still, disappeared over the ridge.

The trail continues the descent, at 1½ miles reaching Lodge Lake, 3125 feet. Pristine! Amid the uproar of high-speed juggernauts, heavy logging, and mechanized recreation, scarcely changed from 1914. Except the trees have added a few inches. And the lodge has been gone half a century.

Here in 1914 The Mountaineers, whose first mountain ascent as a club was Si in 1907, built Snoqualmie Lodge as a base for weekending. Those lucky enough to have a full weekend free would take the streetcar to downtown Seattle to catch the Milwaukee train Saturday (or better, Friday after work or school) and get off at Rockdale Station, the west portal of the Snoqualmie Tunnel. By candle lantern the Friday-nighters would climb the short, steep trail, fire up the wood range (the one that in the 1940s burnt the lodge to the ground), and singsong and hippetty-hop to strains of the accordion. Arise at dawn to climb one or more of the twenty Snoqualmie Pin Peaks. Back at dusk for more jigging and singing. Up Sunday morning to "grab" another peak. Down the trail to the train in dusk and so home. The Snoqualmie Lodge was the birthplace of weekend climbing in the Northwest; from "pin peaks" was to evolve, in the 1930s, the Climbing Course and a mountaineering tradition the equal of any in America.

The lodge made it too much fun to stay home in winter. Ice skating, sledding, and snowball fights led to snowshoe tramps. Scandinavians amused the group with their eccentric snowshoes, not webs but long and skinny boards. The oddity caught on, the Meany Ski Hut was built near Stampede Pass, and the Patrol Race from Snoqualmie Lodge to Meany was a prestigious Northwest competition almost until World War II. Touring (later called "cross-country") was the sport then. But when Seattle Parks Department rigged a rope tow at the pass, Mountaineers began sneaking the trail from Lodge Lake to "Municipal Hill" for the novelty of gaining elevation without effort. No honor, of course, to those pioneering yo-yos. Honor was reserved for ski-mountaineers who toured from the lodge to Olallie Meadows and beyond to the summit of Silver Peak.

EAST OF SNOQUALMIE PASS

Beyond the Cascade Crest, over the hump, into the Mysterious East. . . . Look out for rattlesnakes, stickseeds in your socks. Sunshine broils your brain and makes you vote funny. Where does I-90 go? To Montana, I know for sure from personal travels as an adult. Some say that if you follow it too far, you'll fall off the edge of the world.

Our book puts you at no such risk. Granted, as you descend the east

Air view of Rampart Ridge

slope of the Cascades the delicious rains of God's country may cease and blue holes tatter the clouds, letting through the lethal radiation the ozone layer used to bar. However, the hikes we here describe venture only briefly into sagebrush and sun. The access roads quickly turn off I-90 to return west, to the security of the maritime onshore flow, to peaks that if not on the Cascade Crest are just across the valley and just as wet.

We include these outings because they belong to the inevitable logic of I-90, as much its realm as those that lie minutes by freeway to the west.

However, we can testify from personal experience that the dangers of Central Washington are no more fearsome than commute hour in the Emerald City, and the flowers—O the flowers! For them we recommend to you our *55 Hikes in Central Washington*. Have the book in your car and if on a day of early spring the snow is still up to your neck at the pass or on a day of summer the windshield wiper can't keep up with the onshore flow, darn the stickseeds, the Jubjub bird, and the frumious Bandersnatch—drive on, let the sun shine its worst.

46 | MOUNT CATHERINE

Round trip: 3 miles
Hiking time: Allow 3 hours
High point: 5052 feet
Elevation gain: 1300 feet
Hikable: July–mid-November
Map: Green Trails No. 207 Snoqualmie Pass

We ignored this peak for years because the trail wasn't shown on any maps we'd seen. Ira was checking his collection of 1930s and '40s maps and noted a beacon on top. If there once was a beacon on top, there must be a trail. Finally, while working on *100 Hikes of the South Cascades* he decided to go take a look. The trailhead was easy to find but as he neared the summit the way was lost in deep snow, forcing him to go straight up. But when he got to the "top," it wasn't; there was something higher. Lacking the benefit of a trail, he climbed the second summit, and that wasn't the top either. Discouraging. Nevertheless, onward and upward, until a very steep snow slope persuaded him to go home. A month later he tried again. This time snow had melted from the trail, the false summits could be ignored, the flowers were in bloom, and the views were worth every drop of sweat. But again he was stopped. Not by snow, by big sweet huckleberries. Thinking of you, our readers, he forged ahead to the summit.

The trail is occasionally maintained and is listed in the *Cle Elum District Trail Guide*, but is not on the USGS, Green Trails, or Forest Service recreation

Looking north from the Mount Catherine trail

maps. Why does it exist? An ancient 1930s map shows an airway beacon on the summit, guiding intrepid night-flying birdmen of Lucky Lindy's generation to the low spot on the Cascade Crest (but all too often, sorry to say, not through it). The beacon was one of a line across the country that included others atop McClellan Butte, Rattlesnake Mountain, and West Tiger Mountain. All now gone, along with Joe DiMaggio.

The views south to Rainier and north into the Alpine Lakes Wilderness make Mount Catherine an attractive alternative to boot-busy paths closer to the freeway. However, hikers must deal with two serious obstacles. In early summer, that treacherously steep snowfield may put the final summit off-limits except to ice-ax-equipped climbers (even as it stopped Ira). In late summer, a climber may be ambushed as was Ira by lush blue masses of delicious huckleberries forcing themselves into his mouth.

Drive I-90 east from Snoqualmie Pass 2 miles and go off on Hyak Exit 54. Follow directions 3 miles to the Twin Lakes trailhead (Hike 47), continue to just over 5 miles, and find a small, poor parking space, elevation 3700 feet. Don't be confused by an abandoned road 0.5 mile short of the trailhead.

Trail No. 1348 starts up a rocky, abandoned logging spur to a landing. Cross the landing to true trail and, in two long switchbacks up a 1970s clearcut, enter the forest. A dozen more switchbacks in ¾ mile gain 800 feet to—the top? No, *a* top, but merely of the wooded ridge. With little downs, lots of ups, and a few peekaboo views, the ridge crest continues over more tops. The trees grow smaller, the views bigger, until the way ascends

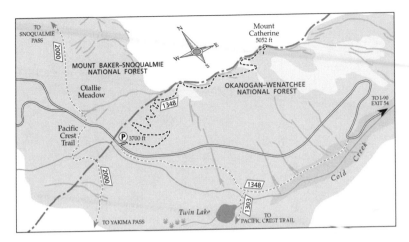

heather clumps past an old cabin site. A cable assists in a final scramble to the genuine rocky top. Gaze north up Gold Creek to the sharp fang of Thompson and the hump of Chikamin Ridge, down 2000 feet to the Lilliput of Snoqualmie Pass and the Tonka toys on I-90. Don't waste much time on the south; from close-by Silver and Tinkham Peaks to the distant vastness of Rainier, the route of the Pacific Crest National Scenic Trail is the clearcut checkerboard of the Northern Pacific Land Grant, bringing to mind the historic exhortation of Horace Greeley, "Go West, young logger."

47 | TWIN LAKE

Round trip: 2 miles
Hiking time: Allow 2 hours
High point: 3180 feet
Elevation gain: 200 feet
Hikable: July–October
Map: Green Trails No. 207 Snoqualmie Pass

A small mountain lake surrounded by forest and mirroring Silver Peak. An easy trail and a shallow beach make it an ideal destination for small children. Twin Lakes they used to be, but over the years the upper lake has evolved in the normal life progression from lake to swamp, ringed by dense walls of shrubbery.

Drive I-90 east from Snoqualmie Pass 2 miles and go off on Hyak Exit 54. Turn right and then left into the large Pacific West Hyak ski area parking lot. Halfway through the lot, go left on a road obscurely signed "Hyak

Twin Lake and Silver Peak

Estates Division 3 and 4." Pass houses and go to the right of the wastewater treatment plant; here the way becomes road No. 9070. At 1 mile is a junction; keep left on No. 9070. At 3.3 miles from I-90 is Cold Creek trail No. 1303, signed "Twin Lakes." Elevation 3029 feet.

While walking the trail, note the difference between the soft-cushion forest floor in stretches of virgin forest and the naked-stone trail in clearcuts. Where did all the topsoil go? It's sure not anywhere around here to grow another crop in the "tree farm." (A clue: look for it somewhere downstream, like, say, the Pacific Ocean.) Clearcuts and forest alternate some ¾ mile to Lower Twin Lake, 3180 feet. Silver Peak stands 2400 feet above.

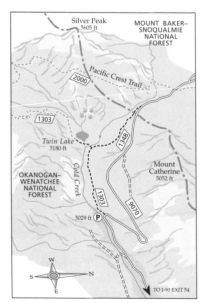

A gravel bar near the outlet of the surviving Twin Lake is good wading; the kids should bring sandals to protect bare feet from sharp rocks and sticks. Watch in the shallows for dippers, the indicators of "healthy water."

With a round trip of just 2 miles and an elevation gain of a mere 200 feet (the one and only) Twin Lake is a fine turnaround for short and/or lazy legs.

48 | COLD CREEK–SILVER PEAK LOOP

Loop trip: 7¾ miles; with peak, 9½ miles
Hiking time: Allow 3½ hours; with peak, allow 6 hours
High point of loop: 4500 feet; of peak, 5605 feet
Elevation gain of loop: 1500 feet; with peak, 2600 feet
Hikable: July–October
Map: Green Trails No. 207 Snoqualmie Pass

Considerable forest survives, and lovely are the trees. The lakes mirror them, and the sky. Summit views are straight down from your toes to Annette Lake, north to Snoqualmie Pass peaks, west to the Olympics, south over motheaten ridges rolling mournfully to Rainier, and east across valley-drowning Keechelus Reservoir to Mt. Margaret, patched by clearcuts as if suffering from terminal mange.

Long gone are the pristinity and remoteness that ranked this among the most popular hikes near Snoqualmie Pass. Few islets of beauty have survived four decades of romping and chomping by the timber companies. Custodian of intervening squares of the Northern Pacific Land Grant checkerboard, the Forest Service sincerely tries to provide "multiple use," and thus there still are trails, as there are not in the horizon-to-horizon clearcuts of "tree farms." Enjoy the sky; there's a lot more of it in cheerful stumplands of "thrifty young forest" than amid the gloom of decadent old giants in ancient-forest cathedrals.

Drive to the Cold Creek trailhead, signed "Twin Lakes" (Hike 47), elevation 3029 feet. (If your sole interest is the up-and-back ascent of Silver,

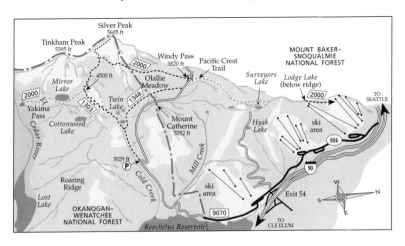

stay on road No. 9070 another 2 miles to the Pacific Crest Trail at Windy Pass, 3820 feet. Walk the Crest Trail south 2 miles to a sidetrail as noted below.)

Alternating between clearcuts and forest, Silver Peak standing nearly half a vertical mile above it all, Cold Creek trail No. 1303 attains Lower Twin Lake in about ¾ mile.

At the lake is a trail junction, the split of the loop. One direction is as good as another; because of a poorly marked junction, we suggest the counterclockwise. Take the right-hand trail No. 1348, climbing 600 feet in 1 mile to rejoin road No. 9070. Walk up the road several hundred yards to Windy Pass, elevation 3820 feet, and go south on the Pacific Crest Trail.

From the Pass the Crest Trail contours under Silver Peak, gaining 600 feet in a long 1 mile. Then (agh! arugh!) a switchback loses some 150 feet. Shortly a well-used sidetrail leads up, gaining 400–450 feet in a scant ½ mile to heather-and-shrub parkland. Follow the flowery ridge crest south about 1 mile to rockslides below Silver Peak, some 4¼ miles from the start. If so

Silver Peak trail

inclined, climb a well-beaten path to the right and then scramble 200 feet of steep felsenmeer to the 5605-foot summit.

Return from the 1-mile sidetrip ascent to the Pacific Crest Trail, continue southward on it another long 1 mile to a 4500-foot high point, and go left on Cold Creek trail No. 1303, dropping 1300 feet in 1¾ miles to Twin Lake. Cross the outlet stream and follow it ¾ mile back to the road and so home.

49 | MIRROR LAKE

Round trip: 2 miles (plus ½-mile each-way road walk)
Hiking time: Allow 1½ hours
High point: 4200 feet
Elevation gain: 800 feet
Hikable: Late June–early November
Map: Green Trails No. 207 Snoqualmie Pass

Two pretty mountain lakes surrounded by forest and meadows, rocky peaks rising above. The short trail is ideal for children, though little legs will need help over rocks and roots.

Drive I-90 to Kachess Lake–Stampede Pass Exit 62. Turn south toward Stampede Pass, pass Crystal Springs Campground, cross the Yakima River, and in 1.1 mile turn right on road No. 5480. At 2.7 miles from I-90 pass road No. 5483 and climb above Roaring Creek to a major intersection at 5.2 miles. Take the second road to the right, circling halfway around Lost Lake. At 7.1 miles is the end of sanely drivable road and the recommended parking, elevation 3600 feet.

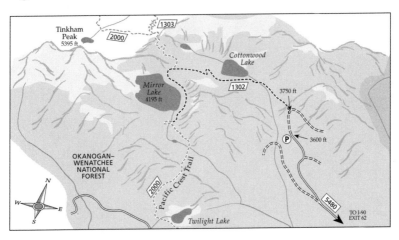

Drive if you dare, or walk ½ mile to the signed trailhead, elevation 3750 feet. The trail plunges through brush of a 1970s clearcut a few hundred feet to forest. With a lot more ups than downs, in ½ mile reach shallow Cottonwood Lake. Not a cottonwood is to be seen. However, ridge-top meadows are in view to the north. For the big picture, continue a long ½ mile to the Pacific Crest Trail, 1½ miles from the recommended parking area.

If you like, go left ¼ mile around the shore of Mirror Lake to the outlet. The rocky summit of Tinkham Peak is reflected in the water. That's the big picture.

Mirror Lake

50 | KENDALL PEAK LAKES

Round trip: 5½ miles
Hiking time: Allow 5 hours
High point: 4790 feet
Elevation gain: 2100 feet
Hikable: July–October
Map: Green Trails No. 207 Snoqualmie Pass

Viewing Kendall Peak from I-90, one never would suspect that below a rugged shoulder lie two delightful lakes and one meadow-ringed pond. What does catch the eye is the 1960s slaughter of the pre-chainsaw forest. Clearcuts stopped only at the boundary of the National Forest, which prevented them from cutting to the shores of the lakes.

Taking the better with the bitter, in Ira's skiing days the logging roads were among his favorite cross-country tours. However, in recent years they have so grown up in brush that there is no room for his archaic snowplow.

Before clearcuts, the lakes had a mythic quality. Climbers looked down on them but seldom went there, save to skinny-dip. The name by which the lakes go derives from the fact that the easiest route to them was over the top of Kendall Peak. The greatest tragedy here, the unkindest cut of all, was the loss of pristine—indeed, untrailed, purely truly wild—forest contiguous with the Alpine Lakes Wilderness. So close above I-90, this would

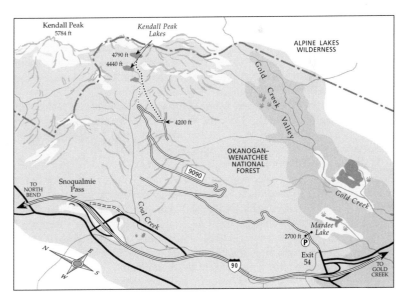

(Lower) Kendall Peak Lake

have been a delight forever to the eye of every freeway passerby from across America. But what did the U.S. Congress and White House of the 1960s know about such matters?

Drive I-90 east 2 miles from Snoqualmie Pass and go off on Hyak Exit 54. On the north side of the freeway, the paved road turns right to Gold Creek. Stay straight ahead on rough dirt road No. 9090, unsigned in 1999, 0.4 mile to a gate and parking area, elevation 2700 feet.

Walk the road, the first mile shaded by trees grown up since the 1960s. As the way climbs, the trees get smaller, this being subeconomic terrain for tree-farming (cut the crop Nature has spent centuries growing and move on, to Canada, Brazil, Siberia, Indonesia). Views of I-90 concrete and ski-area as the clearcuts get bigger. In a long ½ mile from the gate, a spur road goes left. Keep right and pass several more spurs, abandoned. At 2 miles from the gate, the road switchbacks one last time to an end on a 4200-foot knoll. The view here may be sufficient to call it a trip.

However, the forest having become too subalpine-spindly to be worth trucking to mills or docks, the old-time pristine at last lives. Two boot-built paths carry on. The most difficult trail starts back at that last switchback before the final ascent to the knoll. The recommended start is at the knoll. A long ¾ mile leads to the forest-ringed middle lake, 4440 feet. The path steepens to the upper lake, 4790 feet, part of the shore a naked talus from craggy Kendall Peak, where climbers used to come from for dipping.

51 | GOLD CREEK POND

Round trip: 1½ miles
Hiking time: Allow 1 hour
High point: 2490 feet
Elevation gain: None
Hikable: July–November
Map: None needed

Views, yes; wilderness experience, no. A gigantic gravel pit dug to make concrete for I-90. Afterward, the pit area was recontoured and trees, grass, a paved trail, and picnic tables added. It is a park that would do any city proud. The only possible complaint is that it happens to be virtually within the Alpine Lakes Wilderness.

On the east side of Snoqualmie Pass, leave I-90 at Hyak Exit 54. On the

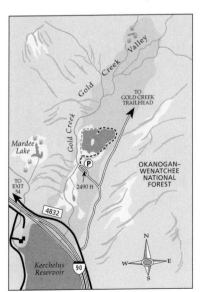

north side of the highway go right on the paved frontage road signed "Gold Creek" for 0.9 mile, then turn left 0.5 mile, and left again to the large Gold Creek Pond (no swimming or boating) parking lot, elevation 2490 feet.

A paved trail leaves near the restroom, skirts a forest, crosses the outlet stream, and in ¼ mile reaches a large picnic area, the ½-mile-wide pond (the old gravel pit), and a circle of views. Starting to the left is 6278-foot Snoqualmie Mountain, then 5784-foot Kendall, the sharp point of 6554-foot Mt. Thompson, 6926-foot Chikamin Peak, and the wide wall of 6400-foot Chikamin Ridge. Continuing the circle is 6151-foot Alta Mountain, followed by the long row of cliffs of 5870-foot Rampart Ridge. In the other direction are the ski runs of Hyak, topped by forested Mount Catherine.

The views don't get any better, but walking the paved path is easy. At this writing the trail ends in ½ mile on the far side of the pond. By the time this book reaches the streets the trail may completely circle the pond.

Cold Creek Pond and Chikamin Peak

52 | GOLD CREEK

Round trip to Alaska Lake: 11 miles
Hiking time: Allow 9 hours
High point: 4200 feet
Elevation gain: 1600 feet
Hikable: Mid-July–September
Map: Green Trails No. 207 Snoqualmie Pass

On the drive east from Snoqualmie Pass, just as you reach Keechelus Reservoir take a quick look north—and don't lose control of the wheel. Up there you'll catch a glimpse of what many consider the beginning of the North Cascades. The headwall of Gold Creek, the loftiness of Chikamin Peak, are a definite notch above any scenery on your drive so far. They speak of higher notches beyond.

Fondly indeed I recall Gold Creek in 1948, my first full climbing season, my first time on a wall way up there in the middle of the air without a rope from above. Nanga Huckleberry! The goats whose skinny path my trembling feet followed up the cliff gasped in admiration. Memories of the Gold Creek trail itself, well . . . there wasn't much to speak of. Exactly beside the highway the loggers had just finished demolishing any trace. Beyond the jackstraw of raw slash a bit of tread led straight into a tumult of raging snowmelt. Hardly out of sight of the car and we'd had two major adventures. On the far side of the torrent the tread almost immediately disappeared under the deep snows of June (this was during the Little Ice Age of the 1940s). Ten miles it was then, 10 wild miles, to Joe Lake, which nowadays I gaze down to from the plush avenue of the Pacific Crest National

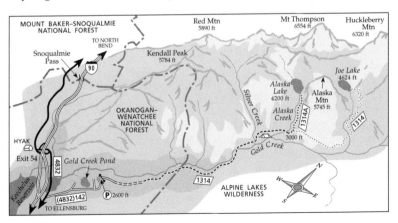

Alaska Lake and Mount Thompson

Scenic Freeway. *Solitude* wilderness commenced, then, a stone's throw from old US 10, a spit of chawin' tobacco from the donkey engine.

However, much good remains. Miles of rushing stream, beneath the cliffs of Rampart Ridge to the east and cliffs of Kendall Peak to the west. Rude steepways to either of two alpine lakes—and to views. To prevent overuse of the lakes, for years the Gold Creek trail has received minimum maintenance, so expect a few blowdowns to be crawled over or wiggled under.

Drive I-90 east 2 miles from Snoqualmie Pass and go off on Hyak Exit 54. On the north side of the freeway follow the former US 10, now a Forest Service frontage road signed "Gold Creek," 0.8 mile. Cross Gold Creek and turn left on road No. (4832)142. In 0.5 mile is a junction. Go straight ahead about 1 mile, avoiding recreation-home sideroads, to a sturdy gate and the beginning of trail No. 1314, elevation 2600 feet. (This trailhead may be moved to Gold Creek Pond—see Hike 51—in 2002, adding ¾ mile each way.)

The first ⅓ mile is an easement on a private driveway, the second ⅓ mile an abandoned road that narrows to a rough trail along the east side of the valley, alternating between woods and avalanche slopes, entering Alpine Lakes Wilderness in 2 miles. At about 3 miles cross Gold Creek (on a footlog or by wading) and continue up the west side of the valley, at about 3½ miles crossing Silver Creek. At 4½ miles cross Alaska Creek; ¼ mile beyond, in a tiny meadow-marsh with views to Alta Mountain and Chikamin Ridge and Peak, is an unmarked junction, 3000 feet.

The left fork climbs 1 steep mile up a tributary through vine maple and slide alder and finally a rockslide to 4200-foot Alaska Lake.

The right fork proceeds up the main valley, contouring and climbing through avalanche greenery, then forest, 1 mile around the base of Alaska Mountain. Traces of the ancient prospectors' path may or may not be found. A steep, hazardous, bootbeaten path on a staircase of rocks and roots ascends to 4624-foot Joe Lake.

53 MOUNT MARGARET–TWIN LAKES–LAKE LILLIAN

Round trip to Twin Lakes: 6 miles
Hiking time: Allow 3½ hours
High point: 5300 feet
Elevation gain: 1500 feet in, 600 feet out
Hikable: Late June–October

Round trip to Lake Lillian: 9 miles
Hiking time: Allow 7 hours
High point: 5300 feet
Elevation gain: 1750 feet in, 750 feet out
Hikable: July–September
Map: Green Trails No. 207 Snoqualmie Pass

Climb a little mountain with big views, then proceed in meadows to a pair of lakelets on the way to roaming Rampart Ridge. Thanks (no thanks) to logging on private land, one must walk a steep, rough road that climbs 1000 feet in the first 2 miles.

Drive I-90 east from Snoqualmie Pass 2 miles and go off on Hyak Exit 54. Follow the frontage road on the north side of the freeway, signed "Gold Creek." At 2.4 miles, near the Rocky Run summer homes, the road becomes No. 4832 and starts abruptly upward. At 3.9 miles go left on road No. 4934. At 4.2 miles is the parking area at the official trailhead, elevation 3800 feet.

The true trailhead has no room to park, so from the "official" one walk 0.2 mile up road No. 4934 and turn steeply uphill left on a gated unmarked road. This land is not your land (due to the Northern Pacific Land Grant) and neither are the roads, which lead in every direction, wherever there used to be trees. Don't count on signs. At 1¾ miles reach the road-end,

Twin Lakes on side of Mount Margaret

drop a few feet, and climb a boot-beaten path into (at last) forest to join what's left of the old Mt. Margaret trail.

Ancient tread ascends to a junction at 2½ miles, near a 5100-foot saddle. Turn left. The trail climbs a bit along the crest, then sidehills the west side of Mt. Margaret. (For views of Margaret, Stonesthrow, Swan, and Rock Rabbit Lakes, leave the trail on one of several boot paths and sidetrip to the

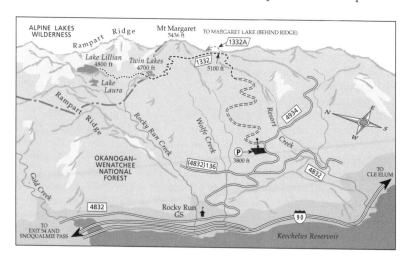

5436-foot summit.) Having rounded the end of the ridge to the north side of the mountain, the trail descends 600 feet to Twin Lakes, shallow ponds in meadows at 3 miles, 4700 feet.

Now the trail gets a bit stern, the tread rough and at times steep as it contours a hillside, losing 150 feet and, after entering the Alpine Lakes Wilderness, gaining 250 feet. At 4½ miles, 4800 feet, is lovely Lake Lillian amid glacier-polished rocks, heather and flowers, and alpine trees.

For off-trail roaming, scramble from the lake to cozy little basins or to broad views atop Rampart Ridge.

54 | MARGARET LAKE

Round trip: 7 miles
Hiking time: Allow 4 hours
High point: 5100 feet
Elevation gain: 1300 feet in, 300 feet out
Hikable: Late June–September
Map: Green Trails No. 207 Snoqualmie Pass

Most lakes in the Alpine Lakes Wilderness are overwhelmed. Margaret Lake is relatively ignored. In the immediate neighborhood, for example, the photogenic cirque of Lake Lillian draws hikers by the regiment while demure Margaret sits lovely and lonesome and quiet in parkland and flowers.

Cirquelet-scoops below the east side of Mt. Margaret hold four sparkling lakes—Swan, Rock Rabbit, Stonesthrow, and Margaret. Once they were connected by well-kept and much-used trails. But two, Swan and Rock Rabbit, have been made unattractive to hikers by logging. Fortunately, Stonesthrow and Margaret are protected in the Alpine Lakes Wilderness. The trail to Stonesthrow has been lost by neglect, but good trail still leads to Margaret.

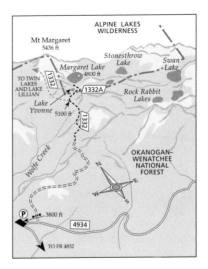

Drive to the Mt. Margaret trailhead (Hike 53), elevation 3800 feet.

Follow the Mt. Margaret route to the 5100-foot saddle, 2½ miles. At the junction go right, switchbacking down. The tread is narrow the

Margaret Lake

first ¼ mile and then becomes wide as the way enters heather/blueberry meadows of the Alpine Lakes Wilderness. In a scant 1 mile from the saddle, the trail passes shallow, spring-fed Lake Yvonne and a bit farther reaches Margaret Lake, 4800 feet, where monster avalanches have swept down from Mt. Margaret, dumping trees and rocks across the lake.

Is it still as lonesome as it was the summer of 1947, when a couple on honeymoon enjoyed appropriate privacy? However, it wasn't what you'd call *quiet*, not with the whine of several trillion mosquitoes. The couple stayed in the water up to their necks as long as possible and upon emerging got quickly and fully dressed. The bride nevertheless came down with a severe case of anemia.

55 | RACHEL LAKE

Round trip: 8 miles
Hiking time: Allow 6 hours
High point: 4650 feet
Elevation gain: 1600 feet
Hikable: Mid-July–October
Maps: Green Trails No. 207 Snoqualmie Pass, No. 208
Kachess Lake

A cool and green valley forest, a large alpine lake walled by glacier-carved cliffs that drop straight to the water, a paradise of rock-bowl lakelets and ponds, gardens of heather and blossoms, and ridges and nooks for prowling. On summer weekends, hundreds of hikers throng Rachel Lake and dozens are in every nook and on every knob of the high ridge, where goats and people have woven a spiderweb of paths.

Drive I-90 east from Snoqualmie Pass 12.5 miles, take Kachess Lake Exit 62, and follow signs 5 miles to Kachess Lake Campground. Turn left 4 miles on Box Canyon road No. 4930 to a junction. Turn left 0.2 mile and hope you can find space for your car in the enormous parking lot at the Rachel Lake trailhead, elevation 2800 feet.

The hike begins with a mile of moderate ascent to a rest stop at water-carved and pot-holed and moss-carpeted slabs. The trail levels out along the creek for 1½ miles. In an open swath of avalanche greenery, look up to 6547-foot Hibox Mountain. At 2½ miles the valley ends in an abrupt headwall. Rough tread proceeds straight up, rarely bothering to switchback, gaining 1300 feet in a cruel mile, the suffering alleviated by glories of cool-breeze rest-stop waterfalls. Suddenly the angle eases and forest yields to meadows and at 4 miles, 4650 feet, is Rachel Lake.

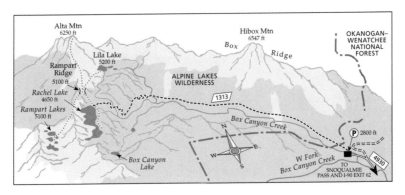

Lila Lake and Hibox Mountain

Follow paths around the lake, admiring blue waters ringed by trees and cliffs. Go left past the narrows to the secluded south bay.

To visit higher country, turn right at the shore on a boot-built path climbing above the cirque, to views down to the lake and out Box Canyon Creek. After a steep ½ mile the trail flattens in a wide parkland saddle, 5100 feet, and reaches an unmarked junction, offering a choice.

Go right 1 mile to 5200-foot Lila Lake (actually two lakes, or maybe six, plus ponds, scattered about a many-level basin) or walk a tightrope in the sky to (or near) the summit of 6250-foot Alta Mountain.

Go left an up-and-down mile to 5100-foot Rampart Lakes. Savor the tiny ponds, the surrounding buttresses and waterfalls. Note the mixture of basalt, conglomerates, and rusty mineralized lobes. Snoop into a flowery corner, climb a heather knoll, think about roaming the short but rough way south to Lake Lillian (Hike 53), and before you know it, arrive on the crest of 5800-foot Rampart Ridge and enjoy views down to Gold Creek, west to Snoqualmie Pass, south to Rainier and Adams, east to Stuart, and north to Three Queens and Chimney Rock.

INDEX

Other titles you may enjoy from The Mountaineers Books:

BACKPACKER'S EVERYDAY WISDOM: 1001 Expert Tips for
  Hikers, *Karen Berger*
Expert tips and tricks for hikers and backpackers selected from
one of the most popular *BACKPACKER* magazine columns.

EXPLORING WASHINGTON'S WILD AREAS: A Guide for
  Hikers, Backpackers, Climbers, X-C Skiers & Paddlers,
  Marge & Ted Mueller
A guide to the undisturbed trails of Washington's federally
preserved backcountry, featuring fifty-five wildernesses and
roadless areas and more than 1000 mapped trails.

HIKING WASHINGTON'S GEOLOGY, *Scott Babcock & Bob
  Carson*
Explores the geologic history of Washington's dramatic landscape.
Four to thirteen hikes are listed for each of the eight different
regions exemplifying the major events that have shaped the area.

100 HIKES IN™ SERIES: The most comprehensive and useful
guides to hiking regions across the United States. These are our
fully detailed, best-selling hiking guides with complete descrip-
tions, maps, and photos. Chock-full of trail data, including access,
mileage, elevation, hiking time, and the best season to go; safety
tips, and wilderness etiquette.
  100 CLASSIC HIKES IN™ WASHINGTON, *Ira Spring &
    Harvey Manning*
  100 HIKES IN™ WASHINGTON'S NORTH CASCADES
    NATIONAL PARK REGION, 3rd Edition, *Ira Spring &
    Harvey Manning*
  100 HIKES IN™ WASHINGTON'S SOUTH CASCADES &
    OLYMPICS, 3rd Edition, *Ira Spring & Harvey Manning*
  55 HIKES IN™ CENTRAL WASHINGTON: Yakima,
    Potholes, Wenatchee, Grand Coulee, Columbia River,
    Snake River, Umtanum, 2nd Edition, *Ira Spring & Harvey
    Manning*
  50 HIKES IN™ MOUNT RAINIER NATIONAL PARK, 4th
    Edition, *Ira Spring & Harvey Manning*
  100 HIKES IN™ WASHINGTON'S ALPINE LAKES, 3rd
    Edition, *Vicky Spring, Ira Spring & Harvey Manning*

THE MOUNTAINEERS, founded in 1906, is a nonprofit outdoor activity and conservation club, whose mission is "to explore, study, preserve, and enjoy the natural beauty of the outdoors . . . ." Based in Seattle, Washington, the club is now the third-largest such organization in the United States, with 15,000 members and five branches throughout Washington State.

The Mountaineers sponsors both classes and year-round outdoor activities in the Pacific Northwest, which include hiking, mountain climbing, ski-touring, snowshoeing, bicycling, camping, kayaking and canoeing, nature study, sailing, and adventure travel. The club's conservation division supports environmental causes through educational activities, sponsoring legislation, and presenting informational programs. All club activities are led by skilled, experienced volunteers, who are dedicated to promoting safe and responsible enjoyment and preservation of the outdoors.

If you would like to participate in these organized outdoor activities or the club's programs, consider a membership in The Mountaineers. For information and an application, write or call The Mountaineers, Club Headquarters, 300 Third Avenue West, Seattle, WA 98119; 206-284-6310.

The Mountaineers Books, an active, nonprofit publishing program of the club, produces guidebooks, instructional texts, historical works, natural history guides, and works on environmental conservation. All books produced by The Mountaineers Books fulfill the club's mission.

Send or call for our catalog of more than 500 outdoor titles:

The Mountaineers Books
1001 SW Klickitat Way, Suite 201
Seattle, WA 98134
800-553-4453
mbooks@mountaineers.org
www.mountaineersbooks.org